Library of
Davidson College

VOID

THE DECADENT CONSCIOUSNESS

A HIDDEN ARCHIVE OF LATE VICTORIAN LITERATURE

FORTY-TWO RARE AND IMPORTANT TITLES
PUBLISHED IN THIRTY-SIX VOLUMES

EDITED BY

IAN FLETCHER &
JOHN STOKES

GARLAND PUBLISHING

STUDIES IN TWO LITERATURES

Arthur Symons

Garland Publishing, Inc., New York & London

1977

Bibliographical note:

This facsimile has been made
from a copy in the
Yale University Library
(Ib50.i897S).

Library of Congress Cataloging in Publication Data

Symons, Arthur, 1865-1945.
  Studies in two literatures.

  (The Decadent consciousness)
  Reprint of the 1897 ed. published by L. Smithers,
London.
  Includes bibliographical references.
  1. English literature--History and criticism--
Addresses, essays, lectures. 2. French literature--
19th cenutry--History and criticism--Addresses, essays,
lectures. I. Title. II. Series.
[PR403.S95 1977]   809   76-20002
ISBN 0-8240-2774-4

Printed in the United States of America

BY THE SAME AUTHOR

DAYS AND NIGHTS: Poems. (*Out of print.*)
SILHOUETTES: Poems. Second Edition. (*Out of print.*)
LONDON NIGHTS: Poems. Second Edition.
AMORIS VICTIMA: A Poem.

STUDIES IN TWO

LITERATURES

STUDIES IN TWO LITERATURES

BY

ARTHUR SYMONS

LEONARD SMITHERS
ROYAL ARCADE: OLD BOND STREET
LONDON W
1897

TO GEORGE MOORE.

My dear Moore,

Do you remember, at the time when we were both living in the Temple, and our talks used to begin with midnight, and go on until the first glimmerings of dawn shivered among the trees, your trees and mine; do you remember how often we have discussed, well, I suppose everything which I speak of in these studies in the two literatures which we both chiefly care about? Our discussions, indeed, never came to an end; for they were the interchange of ideas, the noting, for one another's benefit (or, say, amusement) of sensations; and just because we both wanted to get at the truth of things, and both realized how many aspects truth has, neither of us had the least interest in getting the better of one another in an argument, or in thinking of any argument as finally settled. On first principles we were always, I think, agreed; and how often in regard to individual applications of them! Has either of us ever doubted that a work of art has but one reason for existence, that it should be a work of art, a moment of the eternity of beauty? One forgets, sometimes, that it has entered into the brains of men to doubt anything so obvious. Yet, here they undoubtedly are, critics to whom art means a theory, a belief, a science; the

Ibsenites, the Realists, the Romanticists; people who, when you offer them a rose, say, yes, but it is not a violet. Frankly, I do not understand this limiting of oneself to a school, a doctrine, a costume. I have, and I keep for myself, my own way of seeing things, my own way of trying to say them; you have your own vision of the world, and your own technique. But to you, as to me, whatever has been beautifully wrought, by whatever craftsman, and in whatever manner of working, if only he has been true to himself, to his own way of realizing the things he sees, that, to you as to me, is a work of art; and its recognition, its presentment to other people, who may not immediately have seen it to be what it is, becomes the delightful business of the critic. It is often his privilege to see things before other people; that, you will say, is immaterial; the thing is, to see truly, minutely, and to ignore a defect, rather than to overlook a quality.

That is what I have tried to do in this book, in which I have dealt with many subjects, but with nothing which does not interest me. The essays on Shakespeare are almost the only portions of the book which one could call argumentative; that was a necessity of the case, for I had to clear the ground. Elsewhere, I have combated no opinion; or, if I have, it has been incidentally, or by accident. I have tried to give my own report of whatever I have chosen to consider; I have not even troubled to find out whether it tallies with the reports of other people who have considered the same things. Ah! but I began this letter (did I not?) by assuming that with you, at all events, I should find myself very much in agreement.

I was thinking of our conversations; those conversations which were a kind of intellectual gymnastic, in which we exercised our own apprehensions of things, making them more vivid to ourselves, in the attempt to make them apparent to one another. I think of them now in Rome, where, as in those old times in the Temple, I still look out of my window on a fountain in a square; only, here, I have the Pantheon to look at, on the other side of my fountain. May I, then, in memory of those conversations, dedicate to you my first book of essays in criticism?

Yours as ever,

ARTHUR SYMONS.

ROME, *March* 19*th*, 1897.

The essays contained in this volume were written at intervals during the last ten years; all, with one exception, have been printed in books, magazines, weekly or daily papers; and for permission to reprint them I have to thank Messrs. Blackie and Son (in whose *Henry Irving Shakespeare* most of the Shakespeare essays appeared) and the proprietors and editors of the *Shakspere Quarto Facsimiles*, the *Mermaid Series of Elizabethan Dramatists*, the *Athenæum*, the *Saturday Review*, the *Fortnightly Review*, the *New Review*, *Macmillan's Magazine*, the *Senate*, the *St. James's Gazette*, and the *Savoy*.

CONTENTS

I.—STUDIES IN THE ELIZABETHAN DRAMA

Shakespeare
PAGE
    I. Antony and Cleopatra 3
    II. Macbeth 18
    III. Twelfth Night 28
    IV. Measure for Measure 35
    V. The Winter's Tale 42
    VI. Titus Andronicus and the Tragedy of Blood . 48
    VII. The Question of Henry VIII . . . 69
Philip Massinger 92
John Day 119

II.—STUDIES IN CONTEMPORARY LITERATURE

Christina Rossetti 135
William Morris 150
Coventry Patmore 158
Walter Pater 169
Modernity in Verse 186
A Note on Zola's Method 204

III.—NOTES AND IMPRESSIONS: ENGLISH WRITERS

Richard Jefferies 221
James Thomson 229
Thomas Gordon Hake 236
Robert Louis Stevenson 241
John Addington Symonds 248

IV.—NOTES AND IMPRESSIONS: FRENCH WRITERS

	PAGE
Théophile Gautier	259
Théodore de Banville	264
Henry Murger	273
Benjamin Constant	277
Guy de Maupassant	282
Leconte de Lisle	285
M. Catulle Mendès	288
M. Anatole France	292
M. Huysmans as a Mystic	299
A Symbolist Farce	306

I.

STUDIES IN THE ELIZABETHAN DRAMA

SHAKESPEARE

ANTONY AND CLEOPATRA

Antony and Cleopatra is the most wonderful, I think, of all Shakespeare's plays, and it is so mainly because the figure of Cleopatra is the most wonderful of Shakespeare's women. And not of Shakespeare's women only, but perhaps the most wonderful of women. The queen who ends the dynasty of the Ptolemies has been the star of poets, a malign star shedding baleful light, from Horace and Propertius down to Victor Hugo; and it is not to poets only that her name has come to be synonymous with all that one can conceive of the subtlety of beauty. Before the thought of Cleopatra every man is an Antony, Shakespeare no less than another, though in the play he holds the balance quite steadily. The very name calls up everything that one has read or thought or known of "the world well lost," the giving up of all for love, the supreme surrender into the hands of Lilith, and the inevitable penalty. Probably Shakespeare had had his Cleopatra, though, fortunately for us and for him, he stopped short of the choice of Antony, when

> Entre elle et l'univers qui s'offraient à la fois
> Il hésita, lâchant le monde dans son choix.

But unless we adopt the surely untenable theory that the Sonnets, with their passionate sincerity of utterance, the curiously individual note of their complex harmonies, are merely passion according to the Italian Opera, is it not possible that the dark woman, the "woman coloured ill," of whom they show us such significant hints of outline, may have turned his thoughts in the direction of Plutarch's story of Antony and Cleopatra? It is possible; and if so, Shakespeare must have felt a singular satisfaction in putting thus to use an experience bought so sorrowfully, with so much "expense of spirit;" must have felt that he was repaid, more than repaid.

In the conduct of this play, dealing with so typical a story of passion, and with lovers so unrestrained, it is curious to note how much there is of restraint, of coolness, how carefully the style everywhere is heightened, and how much of gravity, in the scenes of political moment, comes to hinder us from any sense of surfeit in those scenes, the central ones of action and interest, in which the heady passion of Cleopatra spends itself. Never was a play fuller of contrasts, of romantic elements, of variety. The stage is turbulent with movement; messengers come and go incessantly, troops are passing over, engaging, and now in flight; the scene shifts, carrying us backward and forward with a surprising rapidity. But one has a feeling that contrast is of the essence of the piece, and that surprise is to be expected; and not even the variety of the play is more evident than its perfect congruity. Some of this comes about, there can be little question, from the way in which Shakespeare has constructed his play on the very lines of Plutarch, following his authority with a scrupulousness not unlike that of a modern Realist for his "human documents," and no doubt for the same reason. Plutarch was, for Shakespeare, the repository of actual fact; in those pages he found the liveliest image attainable of things as they really happened, and in the comments, outlining the characters, something far more likely to be right than the hazard of any guess of his, so long after. And so fully aware was he of the priceless value of every hint art can extort from nature, of the priceless value of all we can get of real nature, that he was content here to copy merely, to reconstruct after a given plan, and almost without altering a single outline. He gave the outlines life, that was all; and it is a real Antony, a real Cleopatra, that come before us on the romantic stage.

While the main interest of the play is of course centred in the personages who give it name, Shakespeare has not here adopted the device, used in *Macbeth*, for instance, of carefully subordinating all the other characters, leaving the two principal ones under a strong light, and in a salient isolation. He has rather developed these characters through the medium of a crowd of persons and incidents, giving us, not a small corner of existence burningly alive with tremendous issues, but a lover's tragic comedy played out in the sight of the world, on an eminence, and with the fate of nations depending upon it; a tragic comedy in whose fortunes the arrival of a messenger may make a difference, and whose scenes are timed by interviews with generals and rulers. It is the eternal tragedy of love and ambition, and here, for once, it is the love which holds by the baser nature of the man who is the subject of it, the ambition which is really the prompting of his nobler side. Thus the power of Cleopatra is never more really visible than in the scenes in which she does not appear, and in which Antony seems to have forgotten her. For by the tremendous influences which in these scenes are felt to be drawing him away from her, by all that we see and hear of the incitements to heroic action and manly life, we can measure the force of that magic which brings him back always; from Cæsar, who might be a friend, from Octavia, who would be a wife, from Pompey, a rival; to her feet. Such scenes are, besides, a running comment of moral interpretation, and impress upon us a sane and weighty criticism of that flushed and feverish existence, with what is certainly so tempting in it, which is being led by these imperial lovers on terms of such absolute abandonment of everything to the claims of love. This criticism is singularly definite, leaving us in no doubt as to the moral Shakespeare

intended to draw, a moral still further emphasized
by the reticent quietude of Octavia, the counterpoise
to Cleopatra; a character of delicate invention,
surprising us by the precise and attractive image
she leaves upon a play where she is mainly silent.
The ambiguous character of Enobarbus is still
further useful in giving the point of irony which
appears in all really true and fine studies of a world
in which irony seems, after all, to be the final word
with the disinterested observer. Enobarbus acts the
part of chorus. He is neither for nor against
virtue; and by seeming to confound moral judg-
ments he serves the part of artistic equity.

"Antonius being thus inclined, the last and ex-
tremest mischief of all other (to wit, the love of
Cleopatra) lighted upon him, who did waken and
stir up many vices yet hidden in him, and were
never seen of any: and if any spark of goodness
or hope of rising were left him, Cleopatra quenched
it straight, and made it worse than before." So
Plutarch, in the picturesque version of Sir Thomas
North, "Shakespeare's Plutarch," gives the first
distinct sign of the finally downward course of
Antony. Of Antony as he had been, we read a
little above: "Howbeit he was of such a strong
nature, that by patience he would overcome any
adversity: and the heavier fortune lay upon him,
the more constant showed he himself." When the
play opens, this Antony of the past is past indeed;
the first words strike the keynote: "Nay, but this

dotage of our general's." Yet in the character as it comes before us, one finds, broken indeed, yet there though in ruins, the potent nature of the man, standing out now and again suddenly, though with but little result in action. See, for example, in the second scene, the scarcely perceptible flash, in the jesting colloquy with Enobarbus: "No more light words!" and the sudden change which comes about. He can still, when Antony is Antony, command. And observe again, in the meeting between the jarring triumvirs, how gravely and well he holds his own, and especially that scrupulous care of his honour, evidently so dear to him, and by no means a matter of words only. But the man, as we see him, is wrecked; he has given himself wholly over into the hands of a woman, "being so ravished and enchanted of the sweet poison of her love, that he had no other thought but of her." It is in studying Cleopatra that we shall best see all that is important for us to see of Antony.

In the short scene which serves for prelude to the play, we get a significant glimpse of the kind of power wielded by Cleopatra, and the manner in which she wields it. We see her taming with an inflection of frivolous irony the man who has conquered kingdoms; and we see, too, the unerring and very feminine skill, the finesse of light words veiling a strong purpose, by which she works the charm. From the second scene we perceive something of the tremors incident to a conquest held on such terms: the fear of that "Roman thought" which has taken Antony, the little touch of anxiety at his leaving her for a moment. So long as the man is in her presence she knows he is safe. But she has always to dread the hour of departure. And now Antony is going. She plays her spells admirably, but with a knowledge that they will be for once in vain. Her tongue still bites with the scourge of Fulvia: "What says the married woman?" the sneer, a little bitter to say, which comes from a consciousness of the something after all worth having in mere virtue, turned desperately into a form of angry and contemptuous mockery. Antony is not yet dead to honour; he feels his strength, feels that he can break away from the enchantress, as Tannhäuser breaks away from Venus. But Cleopatra knows well that, like Tannhäuser, her lover must come back and be hers for ever.

One sees from the scene which follows how deeply Cleopatra loves, not alone her conquest, but her lover. Hers is a real passion, the passion of a woman whose Greek blood is heated by the suns of Egypt, who knows, too, how much greater is the intoxication of loving than of being loved. There is a passage in one of the *Lettres Portugaises*, and no passage in that little golden book is more subtly true, in which the "learned nun," so learned in the ways of love, pities her inconstant lover for the "infinite pleasures he has lost" if he has never really loved her. "Ah, if you had known them," she says, "vous auriez éprouvé qu'on est beaucoup plus heureux, et qu'on sent quelque chose de bien plus touchant quand on aime violemment que lorsqu'on est aimé." Cleopatra knew this, as she knew everything belonging to the art of which she was mistress. "Us who trade in love," she speaks of frankly, but with perfect self-knowledge; a saying, however, which does her injustice if it leads us to confound her with the Manon Lescauts, exquisite, faithless creatures who keep for their lovers an entirely serviceable kind of affection, changing a lover for a calculated advantage. Love is a "trade" in which she never calculates; wily by nature, and as a loving woman is wily who has to humour her lover, she follows her blood, follows it to distraction, and her fits and starts are not alone played for a purpose, before Antony, but are native to her, and break out with the same violence before her women. She is a woman who must have a lover, but she is satisfied with one, with one at a time; and in Antony she finds her ideal, whom she can call, in her pride, and truly:

> The demi-Atlas of this earth, the arm
> And burgonet of men.

And she loves him with passion real of its kind, an intense, an exacting, an oppressive and overwhelming passion, wholly of the senses and wholly selfish: the love which requires possession, and to absorb the loved one. Before Antony she is never demonstrative : "the way to lose him ! " She knows that a man like Antony is not to be taken with snares of mere sweetness, that neither for her beauty nor for her love would he love her continuously. She knows how to interest him, to be to him everything he would have in woman, to change with or before every mood of his as it changes. And this is her secret, as it is the secret of success in her kind of love. "So sweet was her company and conversation that a man could not possibly but be taken," we read in Plutarch. And Shakespeare has expressed it monumentally in the lines which bring the whole woman before us :

> Age cannot wither her nor custom stale
> Her infinite variety : other women cloy
> The appetite they feed ; but she makes hungry
> Where most she satisfies : for vilest things
> Become themselves in her.

In the fifth scene of the second act we have what is perhaps the most wonderful revelation that literature gives us of the essentially feminine; not necessarily of woman in the general, but of that which radically, in looking at human nature, seems to differentiate the woman from the man. It is a scene with the infinite variety of Cleopatra : it is as miraculous as she : it proves to us that the woman who was "cunning past man's thought" could not be cunning past the thought of Shakespeare. We realize from this scene, more clearly than from anything else in the play, the boundless empire of her caprice, the incalculable instability of her moods, and how natural to her, how entirely instinctive, is the spirit of change and movement by which, partly, she fascinates her lover. The scene brings out the tiger element in her, the union, which we find so often, of cruelty with voluptuousness. It shows us, too, that even in the most violent shock of real emotion she never quite loses the consciousness of self, that she cannot be quite simple. Even at the moment when the blow strikes her, the news of the marriage with Octavia, she has still the posing instinct: " I am pale, Charmian ! " Then what a world of meaning, how subtle a touch of insight into the secrets of the hearts of women, there is in that avowal:

> In praising Antony, I have dispraised Cæsar.
> . . . . . .
> I am paid for 't now.

But when at last, exhausted by the violence of her battling and uncontrollable emotions, she surprises us by those humble words, so full of real pathos:
> Pity me, Charmian,
> But do not speak to me;

one becomes aware of how deeply the blow has struck, how much there is in her to feel such a blow. Certainly, in this as in everything, she can never be quite simple. There is wounded vanity as well as wounded love in her cry. But it is the proudest as well as the most pitiless of women who asks for pity; and one can refuse her nothing, not even that.

It is significant of the magic charm of the "queen, whom everything becomes," and of the magic of Shakespeare's art, that she fascinates us even in her weakness, dominating derision, and winning an extorted admiration from the very borders of contempt. In the scene which follows the flight from Actium, Shakespeare puts forth his full power. There are few more effective groupings than this of Cleopatra sitting silent over against Antony, neither daring to approach the other: he, crushed into an unspeakable shame which can never be redeemed; she, incapable of shame, but seeing it in the eyes of Antony, and conscious that she has done him a deed which can never be forgiven. She is here, as ever, cunning. Excuses can but be useless, and she attempts none, none but the faintest murmur:

> I never thought
> You would have followed!

It is a mere broken sob of "Pardon, pardon!" The tears are at hand, tears being with her the last weapon of all her armoury. They cannot but conquer, and the lover, who has given the world for love, says, not without the saddest of irony, as he takes her kiss: "Even this repays me."

It is in the recoil from a reconciliation felt to be ignoble that Antony bursts out into such coarse

and furious abuse, the first really angry reproaches
he has addressed to her, at the mere sight of
Cæsar's messenger kissing her hand. Despair and
self-reproach have pricked him into a state of smart-
ing sensitiveness. One sees that, as Enobarbus
says, "valour preys on reason"; he is "frighted
out of fear." Well may Cæsar exclaim: "Poor
Antony!" Is there really a cause for his suspicion of Cleopatra? Did she really betray him
to Cæsar? Plutarch is silent, and Shakespeare
seems intentionally to leave it a little vague. But
I think the suspicion wrongs her. Merely on the
ground of worldly prudence she had more to hope
from Antony than from Cæsar. And there is
nothing in all she says to Antony which comes
with a more genuine sound than that reproachful
question: "Not know me yet?" and then, "Ah,
dear, if I be so!"

I have said that Cleopatra has the instinct of
posing. But in Antony, too, there is almost
always something showy, an element of somewhat
theatrical sentiment. Now, preparing for his last
battle, and really moved himself, he cannot help
posturing a little before his servants, exerting
himself to win their tears. It is not a simple
leave-taking; it comes as if prepared beforehand.
And next morning, how stagily, and yet with what
a real exhilaration of spirits, does he arm himself
and go forth, going forth gallantly, indeed, as
Cleopatra says of him! Experience has taught

him so little that he thinks even now that he may conquer. It has been so much his habit, as it has been Cleopatra's (caught perhaps from her) to believe what he pleases! His treatment of Enobarbus shows him still capable of a generous act; a little ostentatious, as it may perhaps be. And the effect of that generous and forbearing tolerance shows that his fascination has not left him even in his evil fortune. He can still conquer hearts. And Cleopatra's? His, certainly, is still hers; and when, raging against the woman who has wrought all his miseries, he learns the news of her pretended death, it is with words full of the quiet of despair that he takes the blow which releases him:

> Unarm me, Eros; the long day's task is done,
> And we must sleep.

Love, as it does always when death has freed us from what we had felt to be a burden, returns; and he stabs himself with the sole thought of rejoining her. When, this side of the grave, he does rejoin her, not a syllable of regret or reproach falls from his lips. In the presence of death he becomes gentle: the true sweetness of the man's nature, long poisoned, comes back again at last. Nothing now is left him but his love for Cleopatra, love refined to an oblivious tenderness; that, and the thought that death is upon him, and that he falls not ignobly:

> a Roman by a Roman
> Valiantly vanquished.

And so the fourth act ends on the magnificent words of Cleopatra over the dead body of the lord of the world and of her. The thought and the spectacle of death, of such a death, call out in her a far-thoughted reflection on the blindness of Fate, the general hazard of the world's course, with a vivid sense of the emptiness of all for which one takes thought. Death takes Antony as a mean man is taken; her, too, he leaves unqueened, a mere woman who has lost her lover. Then "all's but nought," the world is left poor, the light of it gone out; and it is with real sincerity, with a feeling of overwhelming disaster now irretrievably upon her, that she looks to "the briefest end."

In her last days Cleopatra touches a certain elevation: the thought of the death she prepares for herself intoxicates (while it still frights) her reason. It gives her still a triumphant sense of her mastery over even Cæsar, whom she will conquer by eluding; over even Destiny, from which she will escape by the way of death. After all, the keenest incitement to her choice comes from the thought of being led in triumph to Rome; of appearing there, little and conquered, before Octavia. She has lived a queen; in all her fortunes there has been, as she conceived it, no dishonour. She will die now, she would die a thousand times, rather than live to be a mockery and a scorn in men's mouths. How significant is her ceaseless and panging remembrance of

Octavia! a touch of almost petty spite, the spite of a jealous woman. Petty, too (but, inexhaustible as she is in resources, turned, with the frank audacity of genius, into a final triumph) is the keeping back of the treasures. But craft is as natural to her as breath. It is by craft that she is to attain her end of dying. The means of that attainment, a poor man bringing death in his basket of figs, the very homeliness of the fact, comes with an added effect of irony in the passing of this imperial creature. She is a woman to the last, and it is in no heroic frame of mind that she commends the easiness of the death by which she is to die. Yet, too, all her greatness gathers itself, her love of Antony (the one thing that had ever been real and steadfast in the deadly quicksand of her mind) her pride and her tenderness, and, at the last, her resolution.

> I am fire and air; my other elements
> I give to baser life.

So she dies, undisfigured in death, the signs of death barely perceptible, lying

> As she would catch another Antony
> In her strong toil of grace.

And the play ends with a touch of grave pity over "a pair so famous," cut off after a life so full of glory and of dishonour, and taking with them, in their passing out of it, so much of the warmth and colour of the world.

MACBETH

OF all Shakespeare's tragedies, *Macbeth* is the simplest in outline, the swiftest in action. After the witches' prelude, the first scene brings us at once into the centre of stormy interest, and in Macbeth's first words an ambiguous note prepares us for strange things to come. Thence to the end there is no turning aside in the increasing speed of events. Thought jumps to action, action is overtaken by consequence, with a precipitate haste, as if it were all written breathlessly. And in the style (always the style of Shakespeare's maturity) there is a hurry, an impatient condensation, metaphor running into metaphor, thought on the heels of thought, which gives (apart from the undoubted corruption of the text as it comes to us) something abrupt, difficult, violent, to the language of even unimportant characters, messengers or soldiers. Thus the play has several of those memorable condensations of a great matter into a little compass, of which Macduff's "He has no children!" is perhaps the most famous in literature; together with less than usual of mere comment on life. If here and there a philosophical thought meets us, it is the outcry of sensation (as in the magnificent words which sum up the vanity of life in the remembrance of the dusty ending) rather than a reflection, in any true sense of the word. Of pathos, even, there is,

on the whole, not much. In that scene from which
I have just quoted the crowning words, there is,
I think, a note of pathos beyond which language
cannot go; and in the scene which leads up to it,
a scene full of the most delicate humour, the
humour born of the unconscious nearness of things
pitiful, there is something truly pathetic, a pathos
which clings about all Shakespeare's portraits of
children. But elsewhere, even in places where we
might expect it, there is but little sign of a quality
with which it was not in Shakespeare's plan to
lighten the terror or soften the hardness of the
impression one receives from this sombre play.
Terror: that was the effect at which he seems to
have aimed; terror standing out vividly against a
background of obscure and yet more dreadful mystery.
The "root of horror," from which the whole thing
grows, has been planted, one becomes aware, in hell:
do the supernatural solicitings merely foreshow, or
do they really instigate, the deeds to which they
bear witness? Omens blacken every page. An
"Old Man" is brought into the play for no other
purpose than to become the appropriate mouthpiece
of the popular sense of the strange disturbance in
the order of nature. Macbeth is the prey to super-
stition, and it seems really as if a hand other than
his own forces him forward on the road to destruc-
tion. In no other play of Shakespeare's, not even
in *Hamlet*, is the power of spiritual agencies so
present with us; nowhere is Fate so visibly the

handmaid or the mistress of Retribution. In such a play it is no wonder that pathos is swallowed up in terror, and that the only really frank abandonment to humour is in an interlude of ghastly pleasantry, the Shakespearean authorship of which has been doubted.

In this brief and rapid play, where the action has so little that is superfluous, and all is ordered with so rigid a concentration, the interest is still further narrowed and intensified by being directed almost wholly upon two persons. Macbeth and Lady Macbeth fill the stage. In painting them Shakespeare has expended his full power. He has cared to do no more than sketch the other characters. As in one of Michel Angelo's sketches, the few lines of the drawing call up a face as truly lifelike as that which fronts us in the completed picture. But in the play these subordinate figures are forgotten in the absorbing interest of the two primary ones. The real conflict, out of which the action grows, is the conflict between the worse and better natures of these two persons; the real tragedy is one of conscience, and the murder of Duncan, the assassination of Banquo, the slaughters with which the play is studded, are but the outward signs, the bloody signatures, of the terrible drama which is going on within.

When Macbeth, returning victorious from the field of battle, is met by the witches' prediction: "All hail, Macbeth, that shalt be king hereafter!"

is it not curious that his thoughts should turn with such astonishing promptitude to the idea of murder? The tinder, it is evident, is lying ready, and it needs but a spark to set the whole fire aflame. We learn from his wife's analysis of his character that he is ambitious, discontented, willing to do wrong in order to attain to greatness, yet, like so many of the unsuccessful criminals, hampered always in the way of wrong-doing by an inconvenient afterthought of virtue. He has never enough of it to stay his hand from the deed, but he has just sufficient to sicken him of the crime when only half-way through it. He may plan and plot, but at the last he acts always on impulse, and is never able to pursue a deliberate course coolly. He knows himself well enough to say, once:

> No boasting like a fool:
> This deed I'll do before the purpose cool.

Before the purpose cool! that is always the danger to fear, in a nature of this unstable sort. He can murder Duncan, but he cannot bring himself to return and face his work, though his own safety depends upon it. It is the woman who goes back into the fatal chamber, to which he dares not return. No sooner has he done the deed than he wishes it undone. His conscience is awake now, awake and maundering. With the dawn courage returns; he is able to play his part with calmness, a new impulse having taken the place of the last one. Remorse, for the present, is put aside. He plots

Banquo's death deliberately, and is almost gay in hinting it to his wife. Now, his feeling seems to be, we shall be safe: no need for more crime! And then, perhaps, there will be no more of the "terrible dreams."

When Banquo's ghost appears, Macbeth's acting breaks down. He is in the hold of a fresh sensation, and horror and astonishment overwhelm all. After having thought himself at last secure! It is always through the superstitious side of his nature that Macbeth is impressible. His agitation at the sight of the ghost of Banquo is not, I think, a trick of the imagination, but the horror of a man who sees the actual ghost of the man he has slain. Thus he cannot reason it away, as, before the fancied dagger (a heated brain conjuring up images of its own intents) he can exclaim: "There's no such thing!" The horror fastens deeply upon him, and he goes sullenly onward in the path of blood, seeing now that there is no returning by a way so thronged with worse than memories.

Since his initiate step in this path, Macbeth has never been free from the mockery of desire to overcome his fears, to be at peace in evil-doing, to "sleep in spite of thunder." But his mind becomes more and more divided against itself, and the degradation of his nature goes on apace. When we see him finally at bay in his fortress, he is broken down by agitation, and the disturbance of all within and without, into a state of savage distraction, in which the individual sense of guilt seems to be lost in a sullen growth of moody distrust and of somewhat aimless ferocity. He is in that state in which "the grasshopper is a burden," and every event presents itself as an unbearable irritation. His nerves are unstrung; he bursts out into precipitate and causeless anger at the mere sight of the messenger who enters to him. One sees his mental and bodily collapse in the impossibility of controlling the least whim. He calls for his armour, has it put on, pulls it off, bids it be brought after him. He talks to the doctor about the affairs of war, and plays grimly on medical terms. He dares now to confess to himself how weary he is of everything beneath the sun, and seeks in vain for what may "minister to a mind diseased." When, on a cry of women from within, he learns that his wife is dead, he can speak no word of regret. "She should have died hereafter;" that is all, and a moralization. He has "supped full with horrors," and the taste of them has begun to pall. There remains now only the release of death. As prophecy after prophecy comes to its fulfilment, and the last hope is lost, desperation takes the place of confidence. When, finally, he sees the man before him by whom he knows that he is to die, his soldier's courage rises at a taunt, and he fights to the end.

> Nothing in his life
> Became him like the leaving it.

The "note," as it may be called, of Macbeth is the weakness of a bold mind, a vigorous body; that of Lady Macbeth is the strength of a finely-strung but perfectly determined nature. She dominates her husband by the persistence of an irresistible will; she herself, her woman's weakness, is alike dominated by the same compelling force. Let the effect on her of the witches' prediction be contrasted with the effect on Macbeth. In Macbeth there is a mental conflict, an attempt, however feeble, to make a stand against the temptation. But the prayer of his wife is not for power to resist, but for power to carry out, the deed. The same ambitions that were slumbering in him are in her stirred by the same spark into life. The flame runs through her and possesses her in an instant, and from the thought to its realization is but a step. Like all women, she is practical, swift from starting-point to goal, imperious in disregard of hindrances that may lie in the way. But she is resolute, also, with a determination which knows no limits; imaginative, too (imagination being to her in the place of virtue) and it is this she fears, and it is this that wrecks her. Her prayer to the spirits that tend on mortal thoughts shows by no means a mind steeled to compunction. Why should she cry:

Stop up the access and passage to remorse!

if hers were a mind in which no visitings of pity

had to be dreaded? Her language is fervid, sensitive, and betrays with her first words the imagination which is her capacity for suffering. She is a woman who can be "magnificent in sin," but who has none of the callousness which makes the comfort of the criminal; not one of the poisonous women of the Renaissance, who smiled complacently after an assassination, but a woman of the North, in whom sin is its own "first revenge." She can do the deed, and she can do it triumphantly; she can even think her prayer has been answered; but the horror of the thing will change her soul, and at night, when the will, that supported her indomitable mind by day, slumbers with the overtaxed body, her imagination (the soul she has in her for her torture) will awake and cry at last aloud. On the night of the murder it is Macbeth who falters; it is he who wishes that the deed might be undone, she who says to him

> These deeds must not be thought
> After these ways; so, it will make us mad;

but to Macbeth (despite the "terrible dreams") time dulls the remembrance from its first intensity; he has not the fineness of nature that gives the power of suffering to his wife. Guilt changes both, but him it degrades. Hers is not a nature that can live in degradation. To her no degradation is possible. Her sin was deliberate; she marched straight to her end; and the means were mortal,

not alone to the man who died, but to her.
Macbeth could as little comprehend the depth of
her suffering as she his hesitancy in a determined
action. It is this fineness of nature, this over-
possession by imagination, which renders her interesting, elevating her punishment into a sphere
beyond the comprehension of a vulgar criminal.

In that terrible second scene of Act II, perhaps
the most awe-inspiring scene that Shakespeare ever
wrote, the splendid qualities of Lady Macbeth are
seen in their clearest light. She has taken wine
to make her bold, but there is an exaltation in her
brain beyond anything that wine could give. Her
calmness is indeed unnatural, over-strained, by no
means so composed as she would have her husband
think. But having determined on her purpose,
there is with her no returning, no thought of return. It is with a burst of real anger, of angry
contempt, that she cries "Give *me* the daggers!"
and her exaltation upholds her as she goes back
and faces the dead man and the sleeping witnesses.
She can even, as she returns, hear calmly the
knocking that speaks so audibly to the heart of
Macbeth; taking measures for their safety if anyone should enter. She can even look resolutely
at her bloody hands, and I imagine she half believes
her own cynical words when she says:

> A little water clears us of this deed:
> How easy is it then!

Her will, her high nature (perverted, but not subdued) her steeled sensitiveness, the intoxication of crime and of wine, sustain her in a forced calmness which she herself little suspects will ever fail her. How soon it does fail, or rather how soon the body takes revenge upon the soul, is seen next morning, when, after overacting her part in the famous words, "What, in our house?" she falls in a swoon, by no means counterfeit, we may be sure, though Macbeth, by his disregard of it, seems to think so. After this, we see her but rarely. A touch of the deepest melancholy ("Nought's had, all's spent!") marks the few words spoken to herself as she waits for Macbeth on the night which is, though unknown to her, to be fatal to Banquo. No sooner has Macbeth entered than she greets him in the old resolute spirit; and again on the night of the banquet she is, as ever, full of bitter scorn and contempt for the betraying weakness of her husband, prompt to cover his confusion with a plausible tale to the guests. She is still mistress of herself, and only the weariness of the few words she utters after the guests are gone, only the absence of the reproaches we are expecting, betray the change that is coming over her. One sees a trace of lassitude, that is all.

From this point Lady Macbeth drops out of the play, until, in the fifth act, we see her for the last time. Even now it is the body rather than the soul that has given way. What haunts her is the smell and sight of the blood, the physical disgust of the thing. "All the perfumes of Arabia will not sweeten this little hand!" One hears the self-pitying note with which she says the words. Even now, even when unconscious, her scorn still bites at the feebleness of her husband. The will, in this shattered body, is yet unbroken. There is no repentance, no regret, only the intolerable vividness of accusing memory; the sight, the smell, ever present to her eyes and nostrils. It has been thought that the words "Hell is murky!" the only sign, if sign it be, of fear at the thought of the life to come, are probably spoken in mocking echo of her husband. Even if not, they are a passing shudder. It is enough for her that her hands still keep the sensation of the blood upon them. The imagination which stands to her in the place of virtue has brought in its revenge, and for her too there is left only the release of death. She dies, not of remorse at her guilt, but because she has miscalculated her power of resistance to the scourge of an ever-acute imagination.

TWELFTH NIGHT

THE play of *Twelfth Night*, coming midway in the career of Shakespeare, perhaps just between *As You Like It*, the Arcadian comedy, and *All's*

Well That Ends Well, a comedy in name, but kept throughout on the very edge of tragedy, draws up into itself the separate threads of wit and humour from the various plays which had preceded it, weaving them all into a single texture. It is in some sort a farewell to mirth, and the mirth is of the finest quality, an incomparable ending. Shakespeare has done greater things, but nothing more delightful. One might fancy that the play had been composed in a time of special comfort and security, when soul and body were in perfect equipoise, and the dice of circumstance had fallen happily. A golden mean, a sweet moderation, reigns throughout. Here and there, in the more serious parts of the dialogue, we have one of Shakespeare's most beautiful touches, as in the divine opening lines, in Viola's story of the sister who "never told her love," and in much of that scene; but in general the fancy is moderated to accord with the mirth, and refrains from sounding a very deep or a very high note. Every element of the play has the subtlest links with its fellow. Tenderness melts into a smile, and the smile broadens imperceptibly into laughter. Without ever absolutely mingling, the two streams of the plot flow side by side, following the same windings, and connected by tributary currents. Was there ever a more transparently self-contradictory theory than that which removes one or two minute textual difficulties by the tremendous impossibility of a double date? No characteristic of the play is more unmistakable than its perfect unity and sure swiftness of composition, the absolute rondure of the O of Giotto, done at a single sweep of the practised arm. It is such a triumph of construction that it is hard, in reading it, to get rid of the feeling that it has been written at one sitting.

The protagonist of the play, the centre of our amused interest, is certainly Malvolio, but it is on the fortunes of Viola, in her relations with the Duke and Olivia, that the action really depends. The Duke, the first speaker on the stage, is an egoist, a gentle and refined specimen of the class which has been summed up finally in the monumental character of Sir Willoughby Patterne. He is painted without satire, with the gentle forbearance of the profound and indifferent literary artist; shown, indeed, almost exclusively on his best side, yet, though sadly used as a lover, he awakens no pity, calls up no champion in our hearts. There is nothing base in his nature; he is incapable of any meanness, never harsh or unjust, gracefully prone to the virtues which do not take root in self-denial, to facile kindness, generosity, sympathy; he can inspire a tender love; he can love, though but with a desire of the secondary emotions; but he is self-contemplative, in another sense from Malvolio, one of those who play delicately upon life, whose very sorrows have an elegant melancholy, the sting of a sharp sauce which refreshes the palate cloyed by an insipid dish: a sentimental egoist. See, for a revealing touch of Shakespeare's judgment on him, his shallow words on woman's incapacity for love, so contradictory to what he has said the moment before, an inconsistency so exquisitely characteristic; both said with the same lack of vital sincerity, the same experimental and argumentative touch upon life. See how once only, in the fifth act, he blows out a little frothy bluster, a show of manliness, harsh words but used as goblin tales to frighten children; words whose vacillation in the very act comes out in the "What shall I do?" in the pompous declaration, "My thoughts are ripe in mischief," in the side-touches, like an admiring glance aside in the glass at his own most effective attitude, "a savage jealousy that sometime savours nobly," and the like. When he coolly gives up the finally-lost Olivia, and turns to the love and sympathy he knows are to be found in Viola (as, in after days, Sir Willoughby will turn to his Lætitia) the shallowness of his nature reveals itself in broad daylight.

Olivia is the complement to Orsino, a tragic sentimentalist, with emotions which it pleases her to play on a little consciously, yet capable of feeling, of a pitch beyond the Duke's too loudly-speaking passion. Her cloistral mourning for her brother's death has in it something theatrical, not quite honest, a playing with the emotions. She makes a luxury of her grief, and no doubt it loses its sting. Then, when a new face excites her fancy, the artificial condition into which she has brought herself leaves her an easy prey, by the natural rebound, to a possessing imagination. She becomes violently enamoured, yet honestly enough, of the disguised Viola, and her passion survives the inevitable substitution. Shakespeare has cleansed her from the stains of the old story, as he cleansed the heroine of *Measure for Measure*: the note of wantonness is never struck. She is too like the Duke ever to care for him. She has and she fills her place in the play, but the place is a secondary one, and she is without power over our hearts.

We turn to Viola with relief. She is a true woman, exquisitely gracious in that silent attendance upon a love seeming to have been chosen in vain; yet we can find for her no place in the incomparable company of Shakespeare's very noblest women. She has a touch of the sentimental, and will make a good wife for the Duke; she is without the strength of temperament or dignity of intellect which would scorn a delicately sentimental egoist. She is incapable of the heroism of Helena, of Isabella; she is of softer nature, of slighter build and lowlier spirit than they, while she has none of the overbrimming life, the intense and dazzling vitality, of Rosalind. Her male disguise is almost unapparent; she is covered by it as by a veil; it neither spurs her lips to sauciness, as with Rosalind,

TWELFTH NIGHT

nor tames her into infinite dainty fears, as with Imogen; she is here, as she would be always, quiet, secure, retiring yet scarcely timid, with a pleasant playfulness breaking out now and then, the effect, not of high spirits, but of a whimsical sense of her secret when she feels safe in it, coming among women. Without any of the more heroic lineaments of her sex, she has the delicacy and tender truth that we all find so charming: an egoist supremely, when the qualities are his for possessing. She represents the typical female heart offering itself to the man: an ingenuous spectacle, with the dew upon it of early morning. She is permitted to speak the tenderest words in which pathos crowns and suffuses love; and once, under the spell of music, her small voice of low and tender changes rings out with immortal clearness, and for the moment, like the words she says,

> It gives a very echo to the seat
> Where love is throned.

Of Malvolio all has been said, and but little shall be said of him here. He is a Don Quixote in the colossal enlargement of his delusions, in the cruel irony of Fate, which twists topsy-turvy, making a mere straw in the wind of him, an eminently sober and serious man of the clearest uprightness, unvisited by a stray glimpse of saving humour. He is a man of self-sufficiency, a noble quality perilously near to self-complacency, and he has passed the bounds without knowing it. His unbending solemnity is his ruin. Nothing presents so fair a butt for the attack of a guerilla-fighting wit. It is indeed the most generally obnoxious of all tolerable qualities; for it is a living rebuke of our petty levities, and it hints to us of a conscious superior. Even a soldier is not required to be always on drill. A lofty moralist, a starched formalist, like Malvolio, is salt and wormwood in the cakes and ale of gourmand humanity. It is with the nicest art that he is kept from rising sheer out of comedy into a tragic isolation of attitude. He is restrained, and we have no heartache in the laughter that seconds the most sprightly of clowns, the sharpest of serving-maids, and the incomparable pair of roysterers, Sir Toby and Sir Andrew.

Shakespeare, like Nature, has a tenderness for man in his cups, and will not let him come to grief. Sir Toby's wit bubbles up from no fountain of wisdom; it is shallow, radically bibulous, a brain-fume blown from a mere ferment of wits. His effect is truly and purely comic; but it is rather from the way in which the playwright points and places him than from his own comic genius; in this how unlike Falstaff, who appears to owe nothing to circumstances, but to escape from and dominate his creator. Sir Toby is the immortal type of the average "funny fellow" and booncompanion of the clubs or the alehouse; you may meet him any day in the street, with his portly build, red plump cheeks, and merry eyes twinkling at the incessant joke of life. His mirth is facile, contagious, continual; it would become wearisome perhaps at too long a dose, but through a single comic scene it is tickling, pervasive, delightful. Sir Andrew is the grindstone on which Sir Toby sharpens his wit. He is an instance of a natural fool becoming truly comic by the subtle handling in which he is not allowed to awaken too keenly either pity or contempt. In life he would awaken both. He is a harmless simpleton, an innocent and unobtrusive bore, "a Slender grown adult in brainlessness;" and he is shown in all his fatuity without a note or touch of really ill-natured sarcasm. Shakespeare's humour plays round him, enveloping him softly; his self-esteem has no shock; unlike Malvolio, he is permitted to remain undeceived to the end. It is to his credit that he is not without glimmerings that he is a fool. The kindness is, that the conviction is not forced upon him from without.

MEASURE FOR MEASURE

Measure for Measure is neither the last of the comedies nor the first of the tragedies. It is tragedy and comedy together, inextricably interfused, coexistent in a mutual contradiction; such a tangled web, indeed, as our life is, looked at by the actors in it, on the level of its action; with certain suggestions, open or concealed, of the higher view, the aspect of things from the point of view of a tolerant wisdom. The hidden activity of the Duke, working for ends of beneficent justice, in the midst of the ferment and corruption of the seething city; this figure of personified Providence, watchfully cognizant of act and motive, has been conceived by Shakespeare (not yet come to his darkest mood, in which man is a mere straw in the wind of Destiny) to give a sense of security, centred within even such a maze as this. It is not from Isabella that we get any such sense. Her very courage and purity and intellectual light do but serve to deepen the darkness, when we conceive of her as but one sacrifice the more. Just as Cordelia intensifies the pity and terror of *King Lear*, so would Isabella's helpless virtues add the keenest ingredient to the cup of bitterness; but for the Duke. He is a foretaste of Prospero, a Prospero working greater miracles without magic; and he guides us through the labyrinths of the play by a clue of which he has the secret.

That *Measure for Measure* is a "painful" play (as Coleridge called it) cannot be denied. There is something base and sordid in the villany of its actors; a villany which has nothing of the heroism of sin. In Angelo we have the sharpest lesson that Shakespeare ever read self-righteousness.

In Claudio we see a "gilded youth" with the gilding rubbed off. From Claudio's refined wantonness we sink deeper and deeper, through Lucio, who is a Claudio by trade, and without even the pretence of gilding, to the very lowest depth of a city's foulness and brutality. The "humours" of bawd and hangman and the customers of both are painted with as angry a hand as Hogarth's; bitten in with the etcher's acid, as if into the very flesh. Even Elbow, "a simple constable," a Dogberry of the lower dregs, struts and maunders before us with a desperate imbecility, in place of the engaging silliness, where silliness seemed a hearty comic virtue, of the "simple constable" of the earlier play. In the astonishing portrait of Barnardine we come to the simply animal man; a portrait which in its savage realism, brutal truth to nature, cynical insight into the workings of the contented beast in man, seems to anticipate some of the achievements of the modern Realistic novel. In the midst of this crowd of evil-doers walks the Duke, hooded body and soul in his friar's habit; Escalus, a solitary figure of broad and sturdy uprightness; Isabella, "a thing enskied and sainted," the largest-hearted and clearest-eyed heroine of Shakespeare; and apart, veiled from good and evil in a perpetual loneliness of sorrow, Mariana, in the moated grange.

In the construction of this play Shakespeare seems to have put forth but a part of his strength, throwing his full power only into the great scenes, and leaving, with less than his customary care (in strong contrast to what we note in *Twelfth Night*) frayed ends and edges of action and of characterization. The conclusion, particularly, seems hurried, and the disposal of Angelo inadequate. I cannot but think that Shakespeare felt the difficulty, the impossibility, of reconciling the end which his story and the dramatic conventionalities required with the character of Angelo as shown in the course of the play, and that he slurred over the matter as best he could. With space before him he might have convinced us, being Shakespeare, of the sincerity of Angelo's repentance and the rightfulness of his remission; but as it is, crowded as all this conviction and penitence and forgiveness necessarily is into a few minutes of supplementary action, one can hardly think that Coleridge expressed the natural feeling too forcibly in declaring "the strong indignant claim of justice" to be baffled by the pardon and marriage of Angelo. Of the scenes in which Angelo appears as the prominent actor (the incomparable second and fourth scenes of the second act, the first the temptation of Angelo, the second Angelo's temptation of Isabella) nothing can be said but that Shakespeare may have equalled, but has scarcely exceeded them, in intensity and depth of natural truth. These, with that other scene between Claudio and Isabella, make the play.

It is part of the irony of things that the worst

complication, the deepest tragedy, in all this tortuous action, comes about by the innocent means of the stainless Isabella; who also, by her steadfast heroism, brings about the final peace. But for Isabella, Claudio would simply have died, perhaps meeting his fate, when it came, with a desperate flash of his father's courage; Angelo might have lived securely to his last hour, unconscious of his own weakness, of the fire that lurked in so impenetrable a flint. Shakespeare has sometimes been praised for the subtlety with which he has barbed the hook for Angelo, in making Isabella's very chastity the keenest of temptations. The notion is not peculiar to Shakespeare, but was hinted at, in his scrambling and uncertain way, by the writer of the old play on which *Measure for Measure* is founded. In truth, I do not see what other course was open to either in dealing with a situation which was not original in Shakespeare or in Whetstone. Angelo, let us remember, is not a hypocrite: he has no dishonourable intention in his mind; he conceives himself to be firmly grounded on a broad basis of rectitude, and in condemning Claudio he condemns a sin which he sincerely abhors. His treatment of the betrothed Mariana would probably be in his own eyes an act of frigid justice; it certainly shows a man not sensually-minded, but cold, calculating, likely to err, if he errs at all, rather on the side of the miserly virtues than of the generous sins. It is thus the nobility of Isabella that attracts him; her freedom from the tenderest signs of frailty, her unbiassed intellect, her regard for justice, her religious sanctity; and it is on his noblest side first, the side of him that can respond to these qualities, that he is tempted. I know of nothing more consummate than the way in which his mind is led on, step by step, towards the trap still hidden from him, the trap prepared by the merciless foresight of the chance that tries the professions and the thoughts of men. Once tainted, the corruption is over him like leprosy, and every virtue withers into the corresponding form of vice. In Claudio it is the same touchstone, Isabella's unconscious and misdirected Ithuriel-spear, that reveals the basest forms of evil. A great living painter has chosen the central moment of the play, the moment when Claudio, having heard the terms on which alone life can be purchased, murmurs, "Death is a fearful thing," and Isabella, not yet certain, yet already with the fear astir in her of her brother's weakness, replies, "And shamed life a hateful;" it is this moment which Holman Hunt brings before us in a canvas that, like his scene from *The Two Gentlemen of Verona*, is not only a picture but an interpretation. Against the stained and discoloured wall of his dungeon, apple-blossoms and blue sky showing through the grated window behind his delicate dishevelled head, Claudio stands; a lute tied with red ribbons hangs beside him, a rose has fallen on the dark garments at his feet, one hand plays with his fetters (with how significant a gesture!) the other hand pinches, idly affectionate, the two intense hands that Isabella has laid upon his breast; he is thinking, where to debate means shame, balancing the arguments; and with pondering eyes, thrusting his tongue towards the corner of his just-parted lips with a movement of exquisite naturalness, he halts in indecision: all his mean thoughts are there, in that gesture, in those eyes; and in the warm and gracious youth of his whole aspect, passionately superficial and in love with life, there is something of the pathos of things "sweet, not lasting," a fragile, an unreasonable, an inevitable pathos. Isabella fronts him, an embodied conscience, all her soul in her eyes. Her eyes read him, plead with him, they are suppliant and judge; her intense fearfulness, the intolerable doubt of her brother's honour, the anguish of hope and fear, shine in them with a light as of tears frozen at the source. In a moment, with words on his lips whose far-reaching imagination is stung into him and from him by the sharpness of the impending death, he will have stooped below the reach of her contempt, uttering those words, "Sweet sister, let me live!"

After all, the final word of Shakespeare in this play is mercy; but it is a mercy which comes of the consciousness of our own need of it, and it is granted and accepted in humiliation. The lesson of mercy taught in *The Merchant of Venice* is based on the mutual blessing of its exercise, the graciousness of the spirit to which it is sign and seal.

> It droppeth as the gentle rain from heaven
> Upon the place beneath ; it is twice blest ;
> It blesseth him that gives and him that takes.

Here, the claim which our fellow-man has on our commiseration is the sad claim of mutual guiltiness before an absolute bar of justice.

> How would you be
> If He, which is the top of judgment, should
> But judge you as you are ?

And is not the "painfulness," which impresses us in this sombre play, due partly to this very moral, and not alone to the circumstances from which it disengages itself ? For it is so "painful" to think that we are no better than our neighbours.

THE WINTER'S TALE

The Winter's Tale is a typically romantic drama, a "winter's dream, when nights are longest," constructed in defiance of probabilities, which it rides over happily. It has all the licence, and all the charm, of a fairy tale, while the matters of which it treats are often serious enough, ready to become tragic at any moment, and with much of real tragedy in them as it is. The merciful spirit of Shakespeare in his last period, grown to repose now after the sharp sunshine and storm of his earlier and middle years, the delicate art which that period matured in him, seen at its point of finest delicacy in this play and in *The Tempest*, alone serve to restrain what would otherwise be really painful in the griefs and mistaken passions of the perturbed persons of the drama. Something, the very atmosphere, the dawning of light among the clouds at their blackest, at first a hint, then distinctly a promise, of things coming right at last, keeps us from taking all these distresses, genuine as they are, too seriously. It is all human life, but life under happier skies, on continents where the shores of Bohemia are washed by "faery seas." Anachronisms abound, and are delightful. That Delphos should be an island, Giulo Romano contemporary with the Oracles, that Puritans should sing psalms to hornpipes, and a sudden remembrance call up the name of Jove or Proserpina to the forgetful lips of Christian-speaking characters: all this is of no more importance than a trifling error in the count of miles traversed by a witch's broomstick in a minute. Too probable figures would destroy the illusion, and the error is a separate felicity.

It is quite in keeping with the other romantic characteristics of the play, that, judged by the usual standard of such a Romantic as Shakespeare himself, it should be constructed with exceptional looseness, falling into two very definite halves, the latter of which can again, in a measure, be divided. The first part, which takes place in Sicilia, is a study of jealousy; the whole interest is concentrated upon the relations of the "usual three, husband and wife and friend:" Leontes, Hermione, and Polixenes. The jealousy is in possession when we first see Leontes; it bursts forth, flames to its height, almost at once; in its furious heat runs through its whole course with the devouring speed of a race-horse; and then has its downfall, sudden and precipitate, and so dies of its own over-swiftness. Act III, Scene 2, ends the first part of the play; and with the third scene begins the second part, taking us from Sicilia, where the widowed and childless king is left mourning, to Bohemia, where the children, not long born when we last saw Sicilia, are now come to years of love. Then, all through the fourth act, we are with Florizel and Perdita; a sweet pastoral, varied with the dainty knaveries of a rogue as light-hearted as he is light-fingered; the pastoral, too, coming to a sudden and disastrous end, not without a doubtful gleam of hope for the future. With Act V we return to Sicilia, having from the beginning a sense that things are now at last coming to a desired end. Leontes' proved faithfulness, his sixteen years' burden of "saint-like sorrow" gives him the right, one feels, to the happiness that is so evidently drawing near. All does, indeed, fall well, as the whole company comes together at the court of Sicilia, now re-united at last, husband with his lost wife (another Alcestis from the grave) father and mother with child, lover with lover (the course of true love smooth again) friend with friend, the faithful servants rewarded with each other, the worthless likable knave, even, in a good way of getting on in the world.

The principal charm in *The Winter's Tale*, its real power over the sources of delight, lies in the two women, true mother and daughter, whose fortunes we see at certain moments, the really important crises of their lives. Hermione, as we have just time to see her before the blow comes, is happy wife and happy mother, fixed, as it seems, in a settled happiness. Grave, not gay, but with a certain quiet playfulness, such as so well becomes stately women, she impresses us with a feeling, partly of admiration, partly of attraction. It is with a sort of devoted reverence that we see her presently, patient, yet not abject, under the dishonouring accusations of the fool her husband. "Good my lords," she can say,

> I am not prone to weeping, as our sex
> Commonly are; the want of which vain dew
> Perchance shall dry your pities; but I have
> That honourable grief lodged here which burns
> Worse than tears drown. 'Beseech you all, my lords,
> With thoughts so qualified as your charities
> Shall best instruct you, measure me: and so
> The king's will be performed.

All Hermione is in those words, no less than in the calm forthrightness of her defence, spoken afterwards in the Court of Justice. She has no self-consciousness, is not aware that at any time in her life she is heroic; "a very woman," merely simple, sincere, having in reverence the sanctity of wifehood and in respect the dignity of queenship. In Perdita, the daughter so long lost and in the end so happily restored to her, we see, in all the gaiety of youth, the frank innocence and the placid strength of Hermione. She is the incarnation of all that is delightful and desirable in girlhood, as her mother incarnates for us the perfect charm of mature woman. And, coming before us where she does, a shepherdess among pastoral people, "the queen of curds and cream," she seems to sum up and immortalize, in one delicious figure, our holiday loves, our most vivid sensations of country pleasures. It is the grace of Florizel that he loves Perdita; he becomes charming to us because Perdita loves him. In these young creatures the old passion becomes new; and for an hour we too are as if we had never loved, but are now in the first moment of the unique discovery.

This charm of womanhood, this purely delightful quality, of which the play has so much, though it remains, I think, our chief memory after reading or seeing the course of action, is not, we must remember, the only quality, the whole course of the action. Besides the ripe comedy, characteristic of Shakespeare at his latest, which indeed harmonizes admirably with the idyl of love to which it serves as background, there is also a harsh exhibition, in Leontes, of the meanest of the passions, an insane jealousy, petty and violent as the man who nurses it. For sheer realism, for absolute insight into the most cobwebbed corners of our nature, Shakespeare has rarely surpassed this brief study, which, in its total effect, does but throw out in brighter relief the noble qualities of the other actors beside him, the pleasant qualities of the play they make by their acting. With Othello there is properly no comparison. Othello could no more comprehend the workings of the mind of Leontes than Leontes could fathom the meaning of the attitude of Othello. Leontes is meanly, miserably, degradedly jealous, with a sort of mental alienation or distortion, a disease of the brain like some disease of vision, by which he still "sees yellow" everywhere. The malady has its course, disastrously, and then ends in the only way possible: by an agonizing cure, suddenly applied. Are those sixteen years of mourning, we may wonder, really adequate penance for the man? Certainly his suffering, like his criminal folly, was great; and not least among the separate heartaches in that purifying ministry of grief must have been the memory of the boy Mamillius, the noblest and dearest to our hearts of Shakespeare's children. When the great day came (is it fanciful to note?) Hermione embraced her husband in silence; it was to her daughter that she first spoke.

The end, certainly, is reconciliation, mercy; mercy extended even to the unworthy, in a spirit of something more than mere justice; as, in those dark plays of Shakespeare's great penultimate period, the end came with a sort of sombre, irresponsible injustice, an outrage of nature upon her sons, wrought in blind anger. We close *The Winter's Tale* with a feeling that life is a good thing, worth living; that much trial, much mistake and error, may be endured to a happier issue, though the scars, perhaps, are not to be effaced. This end, on such a note, is indeed the mood in which Shakespeare took leave of life; in no weakly optimistic spirit, certainly, but with the air of one who has conquered fortune, not fallen under it; with a wise faith in the ultimate wisdom of events.

TITUS ANDRONICUS AND THE TRAGEDY OF BLOOD

In considering the main question in regard to *Titus Andronicus*, the question of its Shakespearian or non-Shakespearian authorship, it is well to set clearly before us at the outset the actual external evidence which we have. There is, first, the fact that no edition of the play was published during Shakespeare's lifetime with his name on the title-page. On the other hand, it was admitted into the First Folio in company with the mass of his undoubted work. Meres, in his *Palladis Tamia*, published in 1598, refers to it as a genuine play of Shakespeare: "Witness .... for tragedy, his Richard II., Richard III., Henry IV., King John, Titus Andronicus, and Romeo and Juliet." But Ravenscroft, who revived and altered the play in the time of James II, says in his preface to an edition published in 1687: "I have been told by some anciently conversant with the stage that it was not originally his [that is, Shakespeare's], but brought by a private author to be acted, and he only gave some master-touches to one or two of the principal characters."

These conflicting statements have been repeatedly brought into harmony by believers in Shakespeare's entire authorship, part-authorship, and non-authorship, so as to prove that Shakespeare did and did not write the whole play, and that he wrote some part of it. The fact is, they are at the mercy of every theorizer, and can be easily bent to the service of any predetermined hypothesis. The absence of Shakespeare's name from the title, from one point of view a strong proof of an un-Shakespearian authorship, may be met by the obvious cases of *Richard II*,

Richard III, and other unsigned first editions of undoubtedly genuine plays. The attribution of the play to Shakespeare by Meres and the editors of the First Folio, apparently a still stronger proof that he really wrote it, may be almost as easily explained by supposing Ravenscroft's tradition to be true, namely, that Shakespeare revised for the stage a play written by someone else, and that his name thus came to be more and more closely associated with it, until in time it was supposed to be entirely his work. It is on the internal evidence, and the internal evidence alone, that the burden of proof really rests; all that we can require of a hypothesis intelligibly constructed from the evidence of the play itself is, that it shall not be at variance with the few external facts, on a rational interpretation of them.

We know, almost to a certainty, that Shakespeare's earliest dramatic work consisted in adapting to the stage old plays in the stock of his players' company, and very probably in revising new works by unknown and unskilful playwrights. The second and third parts of *King Henry VI* are examples to our hand of the former manner of work: *Titus Andronicus* may with some probability be conjectured to be an instance of the latter. I shall try to show that such a supposition is the least violent and fanciful that we can well make; accepting Ravenscroft's tradition, not from any particular reliance on its probable authenticity, but because, in the absence of any definite information to the contrary, it supplies me with a theory which most nearly agrees with my impressions after a careful examination of the text itself.

Titus Andronicus is a crude and violent, yet in certain respects superior, study in that pre-Shakespearian school which Mr. Symonds distinguishes as "The Tragedy of Blood." This Tragedy of Blood, loud, coarse, violent, extravagantly hyperbolical, extravagantly realistic, was the first outcome of a significant type of Elizabethan character, a hardy boisterousness of nature, a strength of nerve and roughness of taste, to which no exhibition of horror or cruelty could give anything but a pleasurable shock. A popular audience required strong food, and got it.

In the early days of the drama, when playwrights were as yet new to their trade, and without much sense of its dignity as an art, this popular style of tragedy, in the hands of its popular manufacturers, was merely horrible. There were blood and vengeance, strong passions and unrestrained wantonness, but as yet there was no conception of the difference between the horrible and the terrible. Later on, in the hands of Shakespeare and Webster, the old rank Tragedy of Blood, the favourite of the people, became transformed. The horrible became the terrible, a developed art guided the playwright's hand in covering with a certain magnificence the bare and grim outlines of malevolence and murder. It was the same thing, and yet new. The plot of *Hamlet* is the plot of a Tragedy of Blood of the orthodox school, it has all the elements of *The Spanish Tragedy*, but it is fused by imagination, humanized by philosophy, while the ungainly melodrama of Kyd is a mere skeleton, dressed in ill-fitting clothes, but without flesh and blood, without life.

A careful examination of the plays left to us of the period at which *Titus Andronicus* must have been written will show us the exact nature of this species of bloody tragedy, its frequency, and its importance and influence. There may be traced a foreshadowing of it in the copious but solemn blood-shedding of the very first English dramas, the pseudo-classical *Gorboduc* and *The Misfortunes of Arthur*. In these plays, behind the cold and lengthy speeches of the dramatic personages, a wonderful bustle is supposed to be going on. In the argument to *Gorboduc* we read: "The sons fell to division and dissension. The younger killed the elder. The mother . . . killed the younger. The people . . . rose in rebellion and slew both father and mother. The nobility assembled and most terribly destroyed the rebels." In *The Misfortunes of Arthur*, a more loathsome story, filled with murder and rapine, serves as plot to a tragedy of stately speeches. As yet there is no attempt to move by thrilling;

a would-be classical decorum is preserved in the midst of carnage, and the sanguinary persons of the drama comment on their actions with singular gravity. But while the barbarous violence of action is reported as having happened, with a steady suppression of sights and details of blood, it is already potentially present in the background, in readiness for more powerful use by more powerful playwrights.

In *Jeronymo* (or *Hieronymo*) and *The Spanish Tragedy*, in reality a single play of colossal proportions, we have perhaps the first, and at once the foremost, representative of the genuine Tragedy of Blood. The stilted and formal phraseology is still employed, in a much modified and improved form, but there is a real attempt to move the hardy susceptibilities of an audience; the murders occur on the stage, and are executed with much fierceness, and the language of overblown rant is at least intended (and was probably found) to be very stirring. The action of both plays is slow, dull, wearisome, without vivacity or naturalness; the language alternates from the ridiculously trivial to the ridiculously inflated; while in the way of character there are the very slightest indications of here and there a mood or a quality. But the play is important by reason of its position at the head of a long line of tragedies, containing more than one of the dramas of Marlowe, and scarcely coming to an end in the masterpiece of Webster.

The keynote of Kyd's conception of tragedy is murder. Of that most terrible of tragedies, the tragedy of a soul, he is utterly unconscious. Actual physical murder, honourably in the duel, or treacherously by the hand of one of those wonderful villains who live and move and have their being on the Elizabethan stage: this is the very abracadabra of his craft. A fine situation must have a murder or two in it. A troublesome character must be removed by a murder, and the hero and heroine must also be murdered, for the sake of pathos, and a rounded termination, one after the other. Last of all the villain, or the two or three villains, as is more likely, meet with unexpected violent endings, thereby affording a moral lesson of the most practical and obvious kind. In addition there should be a madness, and several atrocities. Madness, only second, though distinctly second, to murder, is an ingredient in many of these plays, notably *The Spanish Tragedy*. It was Hieronymo's madness that attracted that greater poet of the famous "additions," Jonson or another, who, finding it a thing of nought, a conventional, frigidly rhetorical, stage lunacy, left it a thing of pity and terror.

Contemporaneous with *The Spanish Tragedy*, but less representative of the movement, are several other melodramas: the anonymous *Soliman and Perseda*, and Peele's *Battle of Alcazar*, for instance. Becoming, not more human, but more artistic, the

Tragedy of Blood found a willing exponent in the great, daring, but unballasted genius Marlowe, and in the authors of *Lust's Dominion*.

It is to this period that *Titus Andronicus* belongs; a period of more mature art, more careful construction, more power of characterization, but of almost identical purpose. These plays are distinguished from *The Spanish Tragedy* on the one hand, but they are after all still more sharply distinguished from *Lear*, *The Duchess of Malfi*, or even *The Revenger's Tragedy*, and the harsh, powerful dramas of Marston, on the other.

Marlowe's *Jew of Malta* is the most generally known of the Tragedies of Blood, and it is indeed not an ill specimen of the developed style. Marlowe, who originated so much, cannot be said to have originated this manner. It was popular before his time, but, finding in it a certain affinity with his own genius, he attempted it, once, perhaps twice, and in stamping it in his own mint raised its currency. *The Jew of Malta* belongs distinctly to the school of Kyd, but it is raised above its precursors, not only by reason of the frequent splendour of its poetry, but still more by the presence of a finely-imagined character, an idealizing of the passion of greed. The play is Barabas; with his entrance and exit the good in it comes in and goes out. The captains, brutes, and bullies, the shadowy Abigail, all the minor characters, are hasty sketches, rank if not bodiless, mere foils to the malevolent miser. Barabas himself, as it has been so often pointed out, is a creation only in the first two acts, where he foreshadows Shylock; in all the later portion of the play he is only that "monster with a large painted nose" of whom Lamb has spoken. Marlowe and Shakespeare, it is sad to recollect, alike degraded their art, Marlowe more than once, Shakespeare at least once, to please the ears of the groundlings. The intentional debasement of Barabas, in the latter half of *The Jew of Malta*, from a creation into a caricature, is only equalled, but it is equalled, by that similar debasement of Falstaff in *The Merry Wives of Windsor*, from the prophet and philosopher of this world's cakes and ales into an imbecile buffoon, helpless, witless, and ridiculous.

Lust's Dominion, a play issued under the name of Marlowe, but assigned by Mr. Collier, with great probability, to Dekker, Haughton, and Day, is a play of the same class as *The Jew of Malta*, overloaded to an inconceivable extent with the most fiendish crimes, but in several scenes really beautiful and fanciful, and containing, like *The Jew of Malta*, a single predominant character, the villain Eleazar, drawn with abundant strength and some precision. This play is the very quintessence of the Tragedy of Blood; crammed from end to end with the most ingeniously atrocious villanies, but redeemed from utter vulgarity by a certain force and even delicacy of expression, and a barbaric splendour of horror not untinged with ferocious irony. It is a work of art, if of a gross and immature kind, in a sense in which *The Spanish Tragedy* is not. The old outlines remain, but they are filled in with bold but glaring colouring, with coarsely-painted human figures, and are set in a distinct, though loud, key of colour. The thing is revolting, but it is no longer contemptible.

Between these two plays, but rather in company with the former than the latter, I would place *Titus Andronicus*. Like *The Jew of Malta* and *Lust's Dominion*, it contains the full-length portrait of a villain; like *The Spanish Tragedy*, its most powerful scenes are devoted to the revengeful madness of a wronged old man.

In construction *Titus Andronicus* belongs distinctively to the Tragedy of Blood: it is full of horrors and of bloodthirsty characters. There are, if I remember rightly, thirteen murders and executions, besides various outrages and mutilations, in the course of the play. More than half, including a torture and a banquet of human flesh, are enacted on the stage. As regards the characters, there is in Titus a fine note of tragic pathos, in Aaron a certain vigour and completeness of wickedness, in Tamora a faint touch of power, but in Lavinia, in Bassianus, in Saturninus, in the sons of Titus and Tamora, scarcely the semblance of an attribute. The powerful sketch of Aaron is a good deal indebted to the Barabas of Marlowe. There is much the same comprehensive malevolence, feeding on itself rather than on any external provocation; a malevolence even deeper in dye, if less artistic in expression. Both have a delight in evil, apart from the pleasure anticipated from an end gained: they revel in it, like a virtuous egoist in the consciousness of virtue. Eleazar, in *Lust's Dominion*, is a slightly different type of the complete villain. His is a cold, calculating wickedness, not raving nor furious, but set on a certain end. He enjoys his villany, but in a somewhat sad and sober fashion. He is supremely ambitious; to that ambition all other qualities of evil bow, his lust, his cruelty, his spite, his pride; everything. He uses his passions and the passions of others as trained servants; and he sets them tasks, always for his advancement. The three villains, Barabas, Aaron, and Eleazar, are three of the earliest, three primary types, of that long series in which the Elizabethan dramatists attempted to read the problem of Renaissance Italy: of wickedness without moral sense, without natural conscience, wickedness cultivated almost as an æsthetic quality, and attaining a strenuous perfection.

The character of Titus is on a higher plane than that of Aaron; it has more humanity, and a pathos that is the most artistic quality of the play. Titus is the one character, absolutely the only one, who moves us to any sympathy of emotion. The delineation is unequal, there are passages and scenes of mere incoherency and flatness, speeches put into his mouth of the most furious feebleness, but at its best, in the later scenes of half real and half pretended madness, the character of Titus is not so very much below the Hieronymo of the "additions." At its worst it sinks to almost the level of the original Hieronymo. Such curious inequality is not observable in any other person of the play. Aaron and Tamora are the Aaron and Tamora of a single conception, worked out with more or less skill on a level line. The dummies of the play are consistent dummies. Lavinia is a single and unmixed blunder. But Titus, by his situation the most interesting character of the play, is at one time fine, at another foolish, in a way for which it is difficult to account if a single author wrote the whole play.

Lavinia, I have said, is a single and unmixed blunder. There is no other word for it. I can never read the third scene of the second act without amazemeut at the folly of the writer, who, requiring in the nature of things to win our sympathy for his afflicted heroine, fills her mouth with the grossest and vilest insults against Tamora, so gross, so vile, so unwomanly, that her punishment becomes something of a retribution instead of being wholly a brutality. There is every dramatic reason why the victim should not share the villain's soul, every dramatic reason why her situation should be one of pure pathos. Nothing but the coarseness of nature of the man who first wrote it can explain the absurdity. And this is Shakespeare's first heroine, the first of the series which ends with Imogen, in the opinion of those critics who assign the whole of *Titus Andronicus* to the young Shakespeare! The character of Lavinia is alone enough to disprove this opinion; and the character of Lavinia only belongs to the general conception of the play, which is not at all better than might be expected of a clever follower of approved models, a disciple of Marlowe in his popular melodrama. But when we have said this, we have not said everything. The beauty and force of certain passages, and the impressiveness of certain scenes, are so marked, and so markedly above the level of the surrounding work, that we may well hesitate to deny to Shakespeare all part or lot in it.

Two positions I think we are justified in assuming. First, that *Titus Andronicus* is so absolutely unlike all Shakespeare's other early work, that it is, to say the least, improbable that the whole play can be his; and second, that the assumption of a revision by him of another man's work is, on the face of it, quite probable and likely. Shakespeare's first original plays were bright, fanciful, witty, dainty comedies, touched with the young joy of existence, full of irreflective gaiety and playful intellect; nowhere dwelling on things horrible and unpleasant, but rather avoiding the very approaches of anything so serious as tragedy. It was the

Court Comedies of Lyly rather than the Bloody Tragedies of Kyd which influenced the earliest dramatic writings of Shakespeare. *Romeo and Juliet*, a romantic drama with a tragical ending, but not a tragedy in the sense in which *King Lear* is a tragedy, shows us very distinctly the manner in which Shakespeare, even at a much later period than the latest assignable to *Titus Andronicus*, dealt with the sadnesses and incongruities of life, with sorrow, loss, death, affliction, wrong. There is not a touch, not a tone of horror all sorrow resolves itself into " tears of perfect moan;" all tragedy dies upon a song. It is exquisitely pathetic, but there is little hint of the unspeakable pathos of *Lear*. Now *Titus Andronicus* is full of gross horror, sickening with the scent of blood, materially moving. It seems nothing less than impossible that the same hand should have written, first this play, in which the playwright revels coarsely in blood and horror; then *Romeo and Juliet*, in which a tragic story is treated with only a lyrical rendering of the tragedy; then *King Lear*, burdened with an almost intolerable weight of terror, but kept sweet, and pure, and fair by the twin quality of pity. Unless Shakespeare wrote *Titus Andronicus* he never touched tragedy without making it either lyrically pathetic or piteously terrible. And it is only natural to suppose that he never did, and never could have done so.

On the other hand, taking into consideration the differences of workmanship traceable in the play, and the comparative force and beauty of certain parts, it is not impossible that Shakespeare had, if not a hand, at least some finger in it. It is known that he was at one time the "Johannes-fac-totum" of a players' company, and that he was employed in furbishing up old plays for fresh performance. Suppose a new play, by a "private author," written, somewhat clumsily, in a popular style, to be offered to the theatre: what would be more likely than that the thing should be handed over to the dramatic journeyman, young Shakespeare, for brief revision and rectification? Young Shakespeare, little as he may care for the style, has of course to hold himself subservient to the ideals of the original playwright; but he heightens, where he can, the art of the delineations, inserts some passages of far more impressive significance, perhaps almost some scenes, and touches the dead level of the language into something of grace and freshness. Thus we have a stupid plot, a medley of horrible incidents, an undercurrent of feeble language; and, in addition, some powerful dramatic writing, together with bright passages here and there, in which a fresh and living image is expressed finely.

Coleridge's fancy or theory as to Shakespeare's way of dealing with a play in revising it; beginning indifferently, adding only a line here and there, but getting more interested as he went on; applies very well to *Titus Andronicus*. All the first act is feeble and ineffectual; here and there a line, a couplet, a short passage, such as the touch on mercy, or the speech of Titus (I. i. 187-200) puts a colour on the pale outline, and permits us for a moment to think of Shakespeare. But the "purple patches" are woefully far apart. Such entire brainlessness as goes to the making of the very important piece of dialogue between the 270th and the 290th lines of the first scene of the first act, is scarcely to be found throughout the whole play. All the business of the act is confused and distorted; lengthy where it should be short, short where it ought to be extended. There is not a touch in it, probable or possible, of the shaping hand of Shakespeare; of itself the act is enough to disprove his authorship of the complete play.

With the second act there is a decided improvement. Aaron, the notable villain of the piece, makes his first appearance; Tamora blossoms out into the full flower of wickedness; and in the mouths of these anything but idyllic personages we have some of those fine idyllic passages which seem not unlike the early style of Shakespeare. For myself, I can see no touch of Shakespeare in the first lines of the act:

"Now climbeth Tamora Olympus' top," &c.

which some would assign to his account. They are a very tolerable but entirely flagrant imitation of

Marlowe's most rhetorical manner; by no means above the reach of the first author of the play, although, in a sense, above his level. But in some later passages it seems not unpermissible to see the token of Shakespeare's hand. The lines from 80 ("She is a woman, therefore may be woo'd"[1]) onward through a speech or two, have unquestionably a truer ring, a more easy flow and vigour, than the surrounding dialogue. Three lines, a little further on :

> The emperor's court is like the House of Fame,
> The palace full of tongues, of eyes and ears :
> The woods are ruthless, dreadful, deaf, and dull ;

have a genuine impressiveness, and one is almost inclined to refer them to Shakespeare, the more so that they have so much the appearance of an insertion that they could be omitted without the least necessary break in the sense. In the second and third scenes there are several well-known passages, often attributed to Shakespeare : "The hunt is up, the morn is bright and gray," &c. (1-6); the companion piece of the third scene, "The birds chant melody

---

[1] This adage seems to have been popular in Elizabethan times, and is by no means necessarily a Shakespearian sentiment. Beside the exactly parallel passage in the First Part of *King Henry VI*, and the partly parallel passage in *Richard III*, there is another, tolerably close, in *The Birth of Merlin* (I. i.) one of the so-called "Doubtful Plays," but as doubtful, in an opposite sense, as *Othello* :

> For her consent, let your fair suit go on ;
> She is a woman, sir, and will be won.

TITUS ANDRONICUS

on every bush;" and, again, the powerful description of the "barren and detested vale" (91 *et seq.*). None of these are wholly unworthy of Shakespeare's youth. The second passage (scene iii. 10-29, and not by any means ending, as some would have it end, at the 15th line) impresses me as the most melodious and fanciful in the play, and, more than that, a really beautiful interlude. If there is any Shakespeare in the play, this is. But the speech of Tamora (91—108) powerful as it is in some respects, is somewhat less obviously Shakesperian. In the blundering and foolish scene between Tamora and Lavinia, further on in the third scene, there is, in conception and general execution, about as much of Shakespeare as of Bacon; but nine really pathetic lines (158-166) I should like to think Shakespeare's. Lavinia says to Demetrius and Chiron, referring to Tamora, "Do thou entreat her show a woman pity."

Chi. What! would'st thou have me show myself a bastard?
Lav. 'Tis true; the raven doth not hatch a lark:
Yet have I heard (O could I find it now!)
The lion, mov'd with pity, did endure
To have his princely paws par'd all away.
Some say the ravens foster forlorn children,
The whilst their own birds famish in the nest:
O, be to me, though thy hard heart say no,
Nothing so kind, but something pitiful!

The turn of these lines, particularly the last two, is good; and it will be noticed that Tamora's next speech, "I know not what it is: away with her," might even better have come directly in answer to Lavinia's first appeal:

> Do thou entreat her show a woman pity.

The "it" of "I know not what it means" would then naturally refer to the "pity" of the preceding line; as it is, there is some irregularity in such an answer, referring as it does to nothing more direct than, "O be to me . . . something pitiful!" The lines have quite the appearance of an insertion.

The last three acts are far superior to the first two. They are mainly concerned with the wrongs and madness of Titus, which I suspect to have been entered into by Shakespeare with more sympathy than the other parts of the play, and almost throughout dignified and humanized by him. I do not mean to say that Shakespeare wrote all, or most, of the speeches assigned to Titus throughout the play, or even in the last three acts. The touches by which a great poet can raise the work of a small poet from puerility to fineness may be slight and delicate; and are, indeed, far too delicate to be distinguished and emphasized by the critic. Nor is the service, which I suspect Shakespeare to have rendered his predecessor, complete. Not a few empty and rhetorical passages put into the mouth of the suffering hero seem like untouched fragments of the former stuff. If anyone will be at the pains to compare, say the speech of Titus at line 65 (Act III) with the speech of Titus at line 33, he will see,

I cannot but think, a considerable difference; and a glance at the tawdry rant of Marcus, at the close of the second act, will still further emphasize the contrast if compared with, say, the five lines of the same speaker at line 82 of the third act. In all the earlier part of the play, and throughout in perhaps every character but Titus, such touches of Shakespeare as we can distinguish are occasional, and are merely brief additions and revisions of single passages. But in the "magnificent lunacy" of Titus (as Mr. Symonds rightly calls it) there is a note of tragic pathos which seems to me distinctly above the reach of an imitative dramatist of the School of Blood. How much of Shakespeare there is in this latter part of the play it is hazardous to conjecture. We cannot so much point to certain lines, as in the earlier acts, and say, "This reads like Shakespeare;" but we perceive a finer spirit at work, and the keener sense that went to the making or mending of some whole scenes, or main parts of them. Mr. Swinburne has pointed out that the significant arrow-scenes are written in blank verse of more variety and vigour than we find in the baser parts of the play; and these, he adds, if any scenes, we may surely attribute to Shakespeare. I would add some part, by no means all, of the second scene of the fifth act; especially that grimly ironical passage from the 80th line onwards about twenty lines. The first 60 lines of the scene, powerful as they are, have no Shakespearian quality in them: they are directly studied from Marlowe, no doubt by the "private author," who was certainly a disciple of Marlowe, and not without a measure of cleverness. Again, the devilish utterances of Aaron (Act V. sc. i.) some of the most noticeable speeches in the play, are absolutely un-Shakespearian, while distinctly in the manner of Marlowe. Indeed, so closely are they imitated from the confession of Barabas (*Jew of Malta*, Act II. sc. ii.) that we can hardly be surprised at the occasional attribution of the play to Marlowe; worse than foolish as this is on every really reasonable ground. All the ending of the play, the grotesquely horrible dish of human flesh, the tortures, &c., is, of course, entirely due to the original author. Nothing is more clearly and more closely connected with the model Tragedy of Blood; and nothing certainly could be more unlike Shakespeare.

Thus we see, on glancing through the play, that *Titus Andronicus*, in its plot, general conception, and most of its characters, belongs distinctly to the Tragedy of Blood, and, being in these respects inferior to the best of it, may be considered the work of a disciple of the school, not of an acknowledged master; while in certain parts it seems to be lifted above itself, vivified and dignified: a combination which naturally suggests the revision of an inferior work by a superior master. The closer we examine it, the more natural does this view become, and the more probable does it seem that in *Titus Andronicus* we have the work of an unknown writer revised by the young Shakespeare. To consider it the work of an amateur, a disciple of the School of Blood, but not a great writer, raised to its present interesting and imperfect state by Shakespeare's early revision (which is substantially the Ravenscroft tradition) seems to explain the otherwise inexplicable mixture in this singular play of good and bad, twaddle and impressiveness; and seems to explain, on the one hand, why it is so good as it is, on the other, why it is no better. I do not think it is very sensible to try to assign the play, as originally written, to some well-known author of the time, such as Greene or Marlowe, rather than to the "private author." Such resemblances of these writers as occur might naturally be imitations; but to father on Marlowe, in especial, the meaner parts of the play, is a quite gratuitous insult to his memory.

THE QUESTION OF HENRY VIII

Henry VIII was first printed in the Folio of 1623, where it ends the series of "Histories." The main historical authorities were, in the first four acts, Holinshed's *Chronicles;* in the fifth, Foxe's *Acts and Monuments of the Church*, commonly known as *The*

Book of Martyrs. The play is a good deal indebted, directly or indirectly, to a narrative then in MS., George Cavendish's *Life of Cardinal Wolsey*, largely quoted by both Holinshed and Hall, though the book itself was not published till 1641. The play follows its authorities closely, alike in the main course of incident and in the general choice of language; but there are numerous deviations from the chronological order of events.

So far we have dealt with facts: what remains must be but conjecture. It is as well to say frankly that we know with certainty neither who wrote *Henry VIII*, nor when it was written. I shall give, first, the scanty records, the few external facts relating to the play; then, the various theories which have been brought forward as to its date and authorship; not having much hope of being able, finally, to speak myself on all points with the enviable assurance of one whose mind is fully and confidently made up.

The first allusion to a play on the subject of Henry VIII is found in an entry in the Stationers' Registers under date February 12, 1604-5: "Nath. Butter] yf he get good allowance for the Enterlude of K. Henry 8th before he begyn to print it, and then procure the wardens hands to yt for the entrance of yt, he is to have the same for his copy." This play, which Collier "feels no hesitation" in supposing to be the play which we find in the Folio, may more reasonably be identified with the

THE QUESTION OF HENRY VIII

rough and scrambling historical comedy of Samuel Rowley, *When you see me, you know mee; or, the famous Chronicle Historie of King Henrie the Eight, with the berth and vertuous life of Edward Prince of Wales*, which Nathaniel Butter published in 1605. It is a bluff, hearty, violently Protestant piece of work, the Protestant emphasis being indeed the most striking thing about it. The verse is formal, with one or two passages of somewhat heightened quality; the characters include a stage Harry, a very invertebrate Wolsey, a Will Sommers whose jokes are as thin as they are inveterate, a Queen Katharine of the doctrinal and magnanimous order, a modest Prince Edward; with minor personages of the usual sort, and, beyond the usual, a Dogberry and Verges set of watchmen, with whom, together with one Black Will, King Henry has a ruffling scene. The play was reprinted in 1613, in 1621, and again in 1632.

The next allusion which we find to a play on the subject of Henry VIII is in connection with the burning of the Globe Theatre on June 29, 1613. Among the Harleian MSS. there is a letter from Thomas Lorkin to Sir Thomas Pickering, dated "the last day of June, 1613," in which we read: "No longer since than yesterday, while Bourbege his companie were acting at y^e Globe the play of Hen = 8, and there shooting of certayne chambers in way of triumph, the fire catch'd." On July 6, 1613, Sir Henry Wotton writes to his nephew: "Now to let matters of state sleep; I will entertain you at the present with what hath happened this week at the Bank-side. The king's players had a new play, called *All is True*, representing some principal pieces of the reign of Henry the Eighth, which was set forth with many extraordinary circumstances of pomp and majesty, even to the matting of the stage; the Knights of the Order, with their Georges and Garter, the guards with their embroidered coats, and the like: sufficient in truth, within a while, to make greatness very familiar, if not ridiculous. Now King Henry, making a mask at the Cardinal Wolsey's house, and certain cannons being shot off at his entry, some of the paper or other stuff wherewith one of them was stopped, did light on the thatch, where, being thought at first but an idle smoke, and their eyes more attentive to the show, it kindled inwardly, and ran round like a train, consuming, within an hour, the whole house to the very ground." A ballad written on the occasion of "The Lamentable Burning of the Globe Play-House on S. Peter's Day" has for the refrain of every stanza:

> O sorrow! O pitiful sorrow!
> And yet it All is True;

an evident allusion to the title of the play whose performance ended so disastrously. The ballad mentions that

> The fearful fire began above
> By firing chambers too;

and we learn from another stanza that the trial of Katharine formed a part of the action:

> Away ran Lady Katharine,
> Nor waited for her trial.
> Such trial was not in her part;
> Escape was all she had at heart.

In the 1615 edition of Stowe's *Annales*, "continued and augmented by Edmond Howes," we read under date 1613: "also upon St. Peter's Day last the playhouse or theatre, called the Globe, upon the Bankside, near London, by negligent discharging of a piece of ordnance close to the south side thereof, took fire, and the wind suddenly dispersed the flame round about, and in a very short space the whole building was quite consumed, and no man hurt; the house being filled with people to behold the play, viz., of Henry the Eighth: and the next spring it was new builded in far fairer manner than before."

It will thus be seen that in 1613 a play on the subject of Henry VIII was being acted at the Globe under the name of *All is True*. It is described by Sir Henry Wotton as "a new play." Further, it represented "King Henry making a mask at the Cardinal Wolsey's house," where chambers were discharged in his honour, as in the Folio *Henry VIII*, i. iv. (stage direction, after line 49: "Drum and trumpet, chambers discharged"). It also apparently contained a scene in which Katharine was brought to trial. The name *All is True* is perfectly appropriate to the play which we have in the Folio, and in the Prologue there are three expressions which may be taken as references to such a title: line 9: "may here find *truth*, too;" line 18: "To rank our chosen *truth* with such a show;" and line 21: "To make that only *true* we now intend." So far, we have a certain show of evidence, very slight indeed, which might lead us to suppose (in the absence of other evidence to the contrary) that the play *All is True*, acted as a new play at the Globe in 1613, was that which is printed as *Henry VIII* in the First Folio of Shakespeare. There is nothing, however, to tell us that this play of 1613 was by Shakespeare.

Leaving for the present the question of date, we must now consider the more important question of authorship. And here we should premise that the fact of *Henry VIII* having been printed in the First Folio is far from being a conclusive argument on behalf of its genuineness, whole or partial. The editors of the First Folio had an elastic sense of their editorial responsibilities. They admitted *Titus Andronicus* and the three parts of *Henry VI*, which it is practically certain that Shakespeare did no more than revise; as well as *The Taming of the Shrew*, which we know to be a recast of the earlier play *The Taming of a Shrew*. They did not admit *Pericles*, which was published in Quarto under Shakespeare's name, universally recognized at the time as his, and, in the greater part of it, so

THE QUESTION OF HENRY VIII

obviously Shakespearian that its authenticity could not have been seriously doubted.

The first to call attention to the metrical peculiarities of *Henry VIII* was a certain Mr. Roderick, Fellow of Magdalen College, Cambridge, some of whose notes are given in the sixth and posthumous edition of Thomas Edwardes' *Canons of Criticism*, published in 1758. Roderick notes (1) that "there are in this Play many more verses than in any other, which end with a redundant syllable .... this Play has very near *two* redundant verses to *one* in any other Play;" (2) that "the *Cæsuræ*, or Pauses of the verse, are full as remarkable;" (3) "that the emphasis, arising from the sense of the verse, very often clashes with the cadence that would naturally result from the metre." "What Shakespeare intended by all this," he adds, "I fairly own myself ignorant."

Before this, Johnson had observed that the genius of Shakespeare comes in and goes out with Katharine, and that every other part might be easily conceived and easily written. Later, in 1819, Coleridge distinguished *Henry VIII* from Shakespeare's other historical plays as "a sort of historical masque or show-play." Even Knight was forced to acknowledge that the moral which he traces through the first four acts has to be clenched in the fifth by referring to history for it. It was not, however, till 1850 that it occurred to anyone to follow out these clues by calling in question the entire authenticity of the play. In that year the suggestion was made by three independent investigators. Emerson, in his *Representative Men*, treating of Shakespeare, says passingly: "In Henry VIII I think I see plainly the cropping out of the original rock on which his own finer stratum was laid. The first play was written by a superior, thoughtful man, with a vicious ear. I can mark his lines, and know well their cadence. See Wolsey's soliloquy, and the following scene with Cromwell, where—instead of the metre of Shakespeare, whose secret is, that the thought constructs the tune, so that reading for the sense will best bring out the rhythm— here the lines are constructed on a given tune, and the verse has even a trace of pulpit eloquence. But the play contains, through all its length, unmistakable traits of Shakespeare's hand, and some passages, as the account of the coronation, are like autographs. What is odd, the compliment to Queen Elizabeth is in the bad rhythm." In taking it for granted that in *Henry VIII* Shakespeare is to be seen altering an earlier piece of work, rather than working contemporaneously with another dramatist, or allowing his own work to be altered, Emerson simply follows in the line of Malone's investigations into the construction of the three parts of *Henry VI*. It did not lie within his scope to investigate the matter further; the passage, indeed, in which he states his view, is a digression from his main argument. In August of the same year Mr. James Spedding published in the *Gentleman's Magazine* a paper entitled "Who wrote Shakespeare's Henry VIII?" in which he dealt at considerable length with the question of authorship. "I had heard it casually remarked," he says, "by a man of first-rate judgment on such points [Tennyson] that many passages in *Henry VIII* were very much in the manner of Fletcher. . . . I determined upon this to read the play through with an eye to this especial point, and see whether any solution of the mystery would present itself. The result of my examination was a clear conviction that at least two different hands had been employed in the composition of *Henry VIII*, if not three; and that they had worked, not together, but alternately upon distinct portions of it." On August 24, 1850, a letter appeared in *Notes and Queries* from Mr. Samuel Hickson (the writer of an investigation into the authorship of *The Two Noble Kinsmen*, published in the *Westminster Review* of April 1847) stating that he himself had made the same discovery as Mr. Spedding three or four years back, and desiring (he adds) "to strengthen the argument of the writer in the *Gentleman's Magazine*, by recording the fact that I, having no communication with him, or knowledge of him, even of his name, should have arrived at exactly the same conclusion as his own." In 1874 the New

Shakspere Society republished Mr. Spedding's essay and Mr. Hickson's letter, supporting the theory of double authorship by Mr. Fleay's and Mr. Furnivall's application of certain further metrical tests. In a paper read before the New Shakspere Society, November 13th, 1874, Professor J. K. Ingram expressed himself as not so fully convinced that the non-Fletcherian portion of the play was by Shakespeare as that the non-Shakespearian part was by Fletcher. " In reading the (so-called) Shakspearian part of the play I do not often feel myself in contact with a mind of the first order. Still, it is certain that there is much in it that is *like* Shakspere, and some things that are worthy of him at his best; that the manner, in general, is more that of Shakspere than of any other contemporary dramatist; and that the system of verse is one which we do not find in any other, whilst it is, in all essentials, that of Shakspere's last period. I cannot name anyone else who could have written this portion of the play" (*New Shakspere Society's Transactions*, 1874, p. 454). Finally, Mr. Robert Boyle, in an " Investigation into the Origin and Authorship of Henry VIII," read before the New Shakspere Society, January 16th, 1885, attempted to prove that Shakespeare had no share whatever in the play, but that the part formerly assigned to him was really written by Massinger, and that Massinger and Fletcher wrote the play in collaboration. Mr. Spedding had accepted the

THE QUESTION OF HENRY VIII

generally-received date of 1612 or 1613, and suggested that the play may have been put together in a hurry on the occasion of the Princess Elizabeth's marriage (February, 1612-1613); Mr. Boyle contended that the play was not produced till 1616, probably not till 1617, and that it was written to supply the place of *All is True* (possibly Shakespeare's, possibly not) which was destroyed in the Globe fire of 1613.

Such, in brief, are the main theories with regard to the various problems raised by this puzzling play. I have purposely avoided saying much as to the question of date, both because I think there is little to be said, and because this little is rather an inference from, than a support to, whatever theory of authorship we may choose to follow.

That Shakespeare, or that any single writer, did not write the whole of *Henry VIII*, seems to me (to take a first step) practically beyond a doubt. So much we can hardly fail to accept; first, on account of the incoherence of the general action, the failure of the play to produce on us a single, calculated effect; secondly, on the even stronger evidence of the versification. As Hertzeberg remarks, *Henry VIII* is "a chronicle-history with three and a half catastrophes, varied by a marriage and a coronation pageant, ending abruptly with the birth of a child." Spedding rightly notes that "the effect of this play *as a whole* is weak and disappointing. The truth is that the interest, instead of rising towards the end, falls away utterly, and leaves us in the last act among persons whom we scarcely know, and events for which we do not care. . . . The greater part of the fifth act, in which the interest ought to be gathering to a head, is occupied with matters in which we have not been prepared to take any interest by what went before, and on which no interest is reflected by what comes after." It is not merely that there are certain defects in the construction: defects in construction are to be found in nearly every play of Shakespeare. The whole play is radically wanting in both dramatic and moral coherence. Our sympathy is arbitrarily demanded and arbitrarily countermanded. We are expected to weep for the undeserved sorrows of Katharine in one act, and to rejoice over the triumph of her rival, the cause of all those sorrows, in another. "The effect," as Spedding expressively puts it, "is much like that which would have been produced by the *Winter's Tale* if Hermione had died in the fourth act in consequence of the jealous tyranny of Leontes, and the play had ended with the coronation of a new queen and the christening of a new heir, no period of remorse intervening." That Shakespeare, not only in the supreme last period of his career, but at any point in that career at which it is possible that the play could have been written, should be supposed capable of a blunder so headlong, final, and self-annulling, is nothing less than an insult to

THE QUESTION OF HENRY VIII

his memory. It is difficult to believe that any single writer, capable of so much episodical power, could have produced a play in which the point of view is so constantly and so unintelligibly shifted.

This is difficult, but it is impossible to believe that any single writer could have produced a play in which the versification obeys two perfectly distinct laws in perfectly distinct scenes and passages. The unanswerable question is: **Did Shakespeare at any period of his life write verse in the metre of Wolsey's often-quoted soliloquy (iii. 2, 350-372)?** If one may believe the evidence of one's ears, never; nor is the metre so admirable that we can suppose he would take the trouble to acquire it, lacking as it is in all that finer magic, in all that subtler faculty of expression which marked, and marked increasingly, his own verse. The versification of some portions of the play does undoubtedly bear a considerable resemblance to the later versification of Shakespeare. We have thus in one play verse which is like Shakespeare's and verse which is unlike Shakespeare's. The conclusion is inevitable: two writers must have been engaged upon it. Messrs. Spedding and Hickson agreed in dividing the play as follows. To the writer whose versification is like Shakespeare's (and whom they took to be Shakespeare) they assign i. 1, 2; ii. 3, 4; iii. 2 (as far as line 203); and v. 1. The rest of the play they assign to the other author. Mr. Boyle, in his examination of the play, while substantially following this division, assigns to the Shakespeare-like author iv. 1 (rightly, as I think), and also adds to his share i. 4, lines 1-24, 64-108; ii. 1, lines 1-53, 137-169; and v. 3, lines 1-113. Reading the remaining parts of the play, the parts written in the metre of that soliloquy of Wolsey, so markedly unlike that of Shakespeare, we find that the metre is as markedly similar to that of Fletcher. Compare with this passage the following typical passage from one of Fletcher's plays, *The False One*, ii. 1:

> I have heard too much;
> And study not with smooth shows to invade
> My noble mind as you have done my conquest.
> Ye are poor and open; I must tell you roundly,
> That man that could not recognise the benefits,
> The great and bounteous services of Pompey,
> Can never dote upon the name of Cæsar.
> Though I had hated Pompey, and allowed his ruin,
> I gave you no permission to perform it.
> Hasty to please in blood are seldom trusty;
> And but I stand environ'd with my victories,
> My fortune never failing to befriend me,
> My noble strengths and friends about my person,
> I durst not trust you, nor expect a courtesy
> Above the pious love you show'd to Pompey.
> You have found me merciful in arguing with ye;
> Swords, hangmen, fires, destructions of all natures,
> Demolishments of kingdoms, and whole ruins,
> Are wont to be my orators. Turn to tears,
> You wretched and poor seeds of sunburnt Egypt;
> And now you have found the nature of a conqueror,
> That you cannot decline with all your flatteries,
> That when the day gives light will be himself still,
> Know how to meet his worth with humane courtesies.
> Go and embalm the bones of that great soldier;

> Howl round about his pile, fling on your spices,
> Make a Sabæan bed, and place this phœnix
> Where the hot sun may emulate his virtues,
> And draw another Pompey from his ashes,
> Divinely great, and fix him 'mongst the worthies.

This gives, in an extreme form, those characteristics which peculiarly distinguish the verse of Fletcher, and which (it will be seen) distinguish equally the passage of *Henry VIII* to which I have referred, and all those portions of the play already indicated; there is the same abundance of double and triple endings, the same fondness for an extra accented syllable at the end of a line (a characteristic which is inveterate in Fletcher, and of which scarcely an example is to be found in the work of any of his contemporaries), the same monotony, the same clash of metrical and sense emphasis. Emerson, in the passage already quoted, defines admirably the difference between this metre and that of Shakespeare; a difference which is indeed so obvious as to make definition seem unnecessary. It may be doubted whether in the whole of Shakespeare there is such a line as this (iii. 2, 352):

> This is the state of man: to-day he puts forth—

where the double ending is composed of two equally accented syllables. Examples by the score could be cited at a moment's notice from any play of Fletcher's, and from Fletcher's plays alone. May we not therefore feel justified in assigning to Fletcher (in the absence, be it understood, of any distinguishing Shakespearian qualities in the characterization and the language) those portions of the play in which the versification is precisely like that of Fletcher and completely unlike that of Shakespeare or any other known dramatist?

We have now to consider the authorship of the remaining part of the play, the more important part, not only because it contains the famous trial-scene, but because the writer introduced, and doubtless sketched out, the various characters afterwards handled by himself and his coadjutor. Are these characters, we may ask first, worthy of Shakespeare, and do they recall his manner of handling? Is their language the Shakesperian language, the versification of their speeches the Shakespearian versification? Or do the characters, language, and versification seem more in the style of Massinger, or of any other writer?

In looking at the characters in *Henry VIII* we must not forget that they were all found ready-made in the pages of Holinshed. The same might, to a certain extent, be said of all Shakespeare's historical plays; the difference in the treatment, however, is very notable. In *Henry VIII* Holinshed is followed blindly and slavishly; some of the most admirable passages of the play are taken almost word for word from the *Chronicles*; there are none of those illuminating touches by which Shakespeare is accustomed to transfigure his borrowings. Nor does Shakespeare content himself with embellishing: he creates. Take, for example, Bolingbroke, of whose disposition Holinshed says but a few words; the whole character is an absolute creation. Shakespeare's fidelity to his authorities is not so great as to prevent him from rejecting material ready to his hand where such material is at variance with his own conception of a character. For example, Holinshed records a speech of Henry V before the battle. Shakespeare writes a new one, in marked contrast to it. Again, Holinshed gives a speech of Hotspur delivered shortly before the battle of Shrewsbury. Shakespeare puts quite other words and thoughts into Hotspur's mouth. In both cases Holinshed furnished a speech that might well have been turned into blank verse; nevertheless, it was set aside. But in *Henry VIII* Holinshed is followed with a fidelity which is simply slavish.

The character of Katharine, for instance, on which such lavish and unreasoning praise has been heaped, owes almost all its effectiveness to the picturesqe narration of the *Chronicles*. There we see her, clearly outlined, an obviously practicable figure; and it cannot be said that we get a higher impression of her from the play than we do from the history. The dramatist has proved just equal to the occasion; he has taken the character as he found it, and, keeping always very close to his authority, he has produced a most admirable copy, transplanting rather than creating. To speak of the character of Katharine as one of the triumphs of Shakespeare's art seems to me altogether a mistake. The character is a fine one, and it seems, I confess, almost as far above Massinger as it is beneath Shakespeare. But test it for a moment by placing Katharine beside Hermione. The whole character is on a distinctly lower plane of art: the wronged wife of Henry has none of the fascination of the wronged wife of Leontes; there are no magic touches. Compare the trial scene in *Henry VIII* (ii. 4) and the trial scene in *The Winter's Tale* (iii. 2) I should rather say contrast them, for I can see no possible comparison of the two. Katharine's speech is immeasurably inferior to Hermione's, alike as art and as nature. It has none whatever of that packed imagery, that pregnant expressiveness, that vividly metaphorical way of being direct, which gives its distinction to the speech of Hermione. It is, moreover, almost word for word from Holinshed. As for the almost equally famous death scene, I can simply express my astonishment that anyone could have been found to say of it, with Johnson, that it is "above any other part of Shakespeare's tragedies, and perhaps above any scene of any other poet, tender and pathetic." Tender and pathetic it certainly is, but with a pathos just a little limp, if I may use the word, flaccid almost, though, thanks to the tonic draught of Holinshed, not so limp and flaccid as Fletcher often is.

If Katharine is a little disappointing, Anne is an unmitigated failure. That she is meant to be attractive is evident from the remarks made about her in various parts of the play, in which we are told that she is "virtuous and well-deserving," that she is "a gallant creature and complete," that "beauty and honour" are mingled in her, and the like. And what do we see? A shadow, a faint and unpleasing sketch, the outline of one of those slippery women whom Massinger so often drew. She would sympathize with the queen, and her words of sympathy are strained, unnatural in her; she is cunning, through all her affected primness ("For all the spice of your hypocrisy," says the odious Old Lady to her); and in what we see of her at Wolsey's banquet she is merely frivolous. In all Shakespeare's work there is no such example of a character so marred in the making, so unintentionally degraded (after Massinger's inveterate manner) as this of Anne. I would rather think that Shakespeare began his career with Lavinia than that he ended it with Anne.

Turning to the character of Henry VIII, we find a showy figure, who plays his part of king not without effect. Looking deeper, we find that there is nothing deeper to discover. The Henry of history is a puzzling character, but the Henry of a play should be adequately conceived and intelligibly presented. Whatever disguise he may choose to assume towards the men and women who walk beside him on the boards, to us he must be without disguise. As it is, we know no more than after reading Holinshed whether the Henry of the play believed or did not believe, or what partial belief he had, in those "scruples," for instance, to which he refers, not without a certain unction. He is illogical, insubstantial, the mere superficial presentment of a deeply interesting historical figure, who would, we may be sure, have had intense interest for Shakespeare, and to whom Shakespeare would have given his keenest thought, his finest workmanship.

A greater opportunity still is lost in the case of Wolsey. We hear a great deal of his commanding qualities, but where do we see them? Arrogance we see, and craft, but nowhere does he produce upon us that impression of tremendous power, of magnificence, in good and evil, which it is clearly intended that he should produce. Is it credible that the dramatist who, in the shape of a swoln and deluded Falstaff, drives in upon us the impression of the man's innate power with every word that he utters, and through all his buffetings and disgraces, should, with every advantage of opportunity, with such a figure, ready made to his hand, as Wolsey, have given us this merely formal transcript from Holinshed, this "thing of shreds and patches?" How dramatically would Shakespeare have worked the ascending fortunes of the man to a climax; with what crushing effect, and yet how inevitably, brought in the moment of downfall! As it is, the effect is at once trivial and spasmodic, and the famous soliloquies, even, when one looks at them as they really are, but fine rhetorical preachments, spoken to the gallery; fine, rhetorical, moving, memorable, but not the epilogue of a broken fortune, the last words of a bitterness worse than death, as Shakespeare or as nature would have given them. One feels that there is no psychology underneath this big figure: it stands, and then it is doubled up by a blow; but one sees with due clearness neither why it stood so long nor why it fell so suddenly. The events happen, but they are not brought about by that subtle logic which, in *Hamlet* or in *Lear*, constructs the action out of the character, and so enables us to follow, to understand, every change, however sudden and unlooked-for, in the uncertain fortunes of a tormented human creature struggling with the powers of fate and of his own nature.

Now all this, so incredible in Shakespeare, is precisely what we find again and again in his contemporaries, and nowhere more than in Fletcher and Massinger. In Shakespeare, never neglectful of the requirements of the stage, the picturesqueness is made to grow out of the real nature of things: Fletcher and Massinger, only too often, are ready to sacrifice the strict logic of character to the momentary needs of a dramatic spectacle, the stage-interest of sudden reverses. And in all that I have been saying of the character-drawing which we see in this play, little has been said which would not lead us to assign this work, so far beneath Shakespeare, to such fine but imperfect dramatic poets as Fletcher and Massinger.

I have spoken of the evidences of Fletcher's metre which we find in certain parts of the play, evidences which seem scarcely to admit of a doubt. But I confess that the metre and language of the non-Fletcherian portion do not seem to me by any means so clearly assignable to Massinger. Massinger's verse is a close imitation of the later verse of Shakespeare; but it is an imitation which stops short at the end of no very lengthy a tether. The verse of the non-Fletcherian portion of *Henry VIII* rings neither true Shakespeare nor true Massinger, and I know of no other dramatist to whom it can be attributed. There are lines and passages which, if I came across them in an anonymous play, I should assign without hesitation to Massinger; there are also lines and passages to which I can recollect no parallel in all his works. Mr. Boyle, in his valuable paper already quoted, gives a certain number of "parallel passages" in support of the Massinger authorship, but I cannot say that they appear to me altogether conclusive. Nor is the argument from supposed historical allusions, by which he assigns the play to 1616 or 1617, a date which would favour the theory that Massinger and Fletcher wrote together, anything more than vaguely conjectural. As I have said before, we really do not know when this play was written; there is nothing to forbid the assumption that it was a new play in 1613, there is nothing to forbid the assumption that it was not written till 1616 or 1617. The backward limit of date is indeed fixed by the characteristics of the metre; but the very slight evidence which identifies the play of *Henry VIII* as we have it, with the play *All is True*, which was being performed on the occasion of the Globe fire, is not conclusive enough to stand in the way of a later date, should a later date seem to be demanded by other considerations. We are thus free to deal with the question of authorship entirely on internal evidence. I have already given my reasons for believing that Shakespeare wrote neither the whole nor a part of the play, and that Fletcher did write certain portions of it. But I cannot hold with any assurance that the second author has yet been discovered. It seems not improbable that this second author was Massinger. But it is far from certain, and, at present, a definite judgment on this point would be premature.

PHILIP MASSINGER

Philip Massinger was born at Salisbury, and was baptized at St. Thomas's on the 24th November, 1583; he died at London, in his house on the Bankside, and was buried in St. Saviour's on the 18th March, 1638. His father, Arthur Massinger, was a retainer of the Herbert family, in whose service, we learn from the dedication of *The Bondman*, he "happily spent many years, and died a servant to it." The exact significance of the word "servant," used many times in reference to Arthur Massinger's position, is not quite clear; it certainly represents an honourable form of service. Evidence of the respect in which the elder Massinger was held may be found in the letters and despatches of Henry, Earl of Pembroke. One of these, addressed to Lord Burghley, recommends him for the reversion of the office of Examiner in the Court of the Marches of Wales; another refers to him as negotiator in a treaty of marriage between the Pembroke and Burghley families; yet another describes him as the bearer of letters from Pembroke to the Queen. It has been conjectured that Philip Massinger may himself have been page to the Countess of Pembroke at Wilton, and imaginative historians are pleased to fancy Sir Philip Sidney as his possible godfather. Life at the most cultured and refined house in England, if such favour was indeed granted him, would acquaint the future painter of courtly manners with the minutest details of his subject; and in some of the men and women who met at Wilton he would see the ideal of manly chivalry, and a higher than the ideal of womanly virtue, to which his writings were to bear witness.

The first authentic account of Massinger, after the register of his baptism, is the entry of "Phillippus Massinger, Sarisburiensis, generosi filius, nat. an. 18" (Philip Massinger, of Salisbury, the son of a gentleman, aged 18) as a commoner of St. Alban's Hall, Oxford, May 14th, 1602. Wood tells us that "he gave his mind more to poetry and romances for about four years or more, than to logic and philosophy, which he ought to have done, as he was patronized to that end" by the Earl of Pembroke. Langbaine, on the other hand, asserts that he closely pursued his studies for three or four years, and that he was supported solely by his father. It is difficult for a reader of Massinger to help believing that logic and philosophy alternated pretty evenly with poetry and romances. Massinger's Latin, by no means despicable, though it has a tendency to concentrate itself in the very serviceable phrase *Nil ultra*, scarcely suggests the temper of a scholar; but that passionate fondness for argument, and intense devotion to principles in the abstract, visible in every page of his works, would consort very ill with the character of the heedless loiterer on learning indicated to us by Wood. In 1606 he quitted the University abruptly, and without taking a degree. About the same time occurred (it is believed) the death of his father; it has been suggested, on the one hand, that he was by this circumstance deprived of his support (supposing it to have been provided by his father); on the other, somewhat fancifully, that "his father's death bereft him of the heart and hope of his academical studies." But if we believe Wood's account, his exhibition was from the Earl of Pembroke. The old Earl Henry, Arthur Massinger's patron, had died on January 19, 1601. Philip Massinger, therefore, who went to Oxford more than a year after Earl Henry's death, would owe his support to William (the supposed "Mr. W. H." of Shakespeare's Sonnets), eldest son and successor of the old earl.[1] Why should this support be suddenly and finally withdrawn? Earl William, we are told by Clarendon, was "the most universally beloved and esteemed of any man of that age . . . of a pleasant and facetious humour, and a disposi-

[1] The Countess of Pembroke, though living at the time, had been left by her husband so badly provided for, that any assistance from her would be quite out of the question.

tion generous and munificent . . . ready to promote the pretences of the worthy." Why then should he have ceased to promote the "pretences" of such a man as Philip Massinger, the son of one of his father's most trusted retainers? It is conjectured by Gifford that Massinger, "during his residence in the University, had exchanged the religion of his father for one at that time the object of terror, persecution, and hatred," and had, by becoming a Roman Catholic, alienated the sympathies of the Earl of Pembroke, who is known to have professed a zealous and patriotic Protestantism. "He was a great lover of his country," says Clarendon, "and of the religion and justice which he believed could only support it; *and his friendships were only with men of these principles.*" In support of his hypothesis, Gifford points particularly to *The Virgin Martyr*, *The Renegado*, and *The Maid of Honour*. I cannot think the evidence of these plays conclusive; but, such as it is, it certainly goes a long way in favour of the supposition. Besides the ecclesiastical legends, the curious conversions of *The Virgin Martyr*, the implied belief in baptismal regeneration, and the wonder-working Jesuit of *The Renegado*, Massinger's view of life and tone of moralizing, not in these plays alone, are far removed from the Puritan standpoint, while distinctly and indeed assertively religious. The Roman Catholic religion would naturally have considerable attraction for a man of Massinger's temperament; and he would certainly have every opportunity of association with it in a University of such Catholic and conservative principles as Oxford.

After leaving the University in 1606, Massinger appears to have gone to London, where, according to Antony Wood, "being sufficiently famed for several specimens of wit, he betook himself to writing plays." The English drama was now at its height; Shakespeare was producing his latest and greatest tragic masterpieces; Jonson, Chapman, Dekker, Middleton, and perhaps Marston, were at their best; Webster was nearing his artistic maturity, and Tourneur flaming out in his sudden phase of short-lived brilliance; Beaumont and Fletcher were about to begin their career. When and how Massinger began to write we are not aware: probably, like most playwrights of the time, he began with adaptation. The first mention of his name as a dramatist occurs in the year 1621, when his comedy *The Woman's Plot* (the play known to us under the name of *A Very Woman*) was performed at Court. During this period of fifteen years he probably produced seven plays, now lost to us through Mr. Warburton's insatiable cook;[1]

[1] The plays in Warburton's possession, burnt leaf by leaf by his cook as covers for pie-crust, were the following: *Minerva's Sacrifice, or, the Forced Lady* (tragedy); *The Noble Choice, or, The Orator* (comedy); *The Wandering Lovers, or, The Painter* (comedy, by Massinger and Fletcher); *Philenzo and Hippolita* (tragi-comedy, altered by Massinger); *Antonio and Vallia* (comedy, altered by Massinger); *The Tyrant* (tragedy); and *Fast and Welcome* (comedy).

several others in collaboration with Fletcher;[1] and *The Virgin Martyr*, *The Fatal Dowry*, *The Unnatural Combat*, and *The Duke of Milan*. It may be doubted whether Massinger was ever sufficiently popular to make a very good living out of his profession of playwright. We have evidence, in the pitiful document discovered by Malone in the archives of Dulwich College, that in the early part of his career he was reduced to beg urgently for an immediate loan of £5. The document is undated; but it is assigned by Mr. Collier to 1624 or the previous year.

After this melancholy flash of light into the darkness of a somewhat shadowy existence, we learn nothing more of Massinger's personal history up to the time of his death, with the exception of the dates of the licensing of his plays, a few allusions to them, and an inference or two which may be drawn from their dedications. It is interesting to know that Henrietta Maria paid Massinger the unusual compliment of attending the performance of his lost tragedy *Cleander* (produced May 7th, 1634); and that another play now lost, *The King and the Subject*, having been referred by the Master of the Revels to the decision of Charles, the king gave judgment in its favour, contenting himself with striking out a single

[1] The plays written by Massinger and Fletcher together (mostly near about this period) are probably not less than thirteen or fourteen.

passage touching too closely on the burning question of Ship-Money, with the words, "This is too insolent, and to be changed."

On the morning of the 17th of March, 1638, Massinger, who had gone to bed on the previous night in apparent health, was found dead in his house on the Bankside. He was buried in St. Saviour's, Southwark; the entry of his interment reads: "1638. March 18th. Philip Massinger, stranger, in the church . . . 2 li." The word "stranger," pathetic as it now sounds, meant nothing more than non-parishioner; and it has been supposed that this fact accounts for the unusual amount of the charge, £2, or double that entered twelve years earlier in the register of the same church for "John Fletcher, a poet." It is said by Sir Aston Cockayne, in his "Epitaph on Mr. John Fletcher and Mr. Philip Massinger," that Massinger and Fletcher, friends and comrades in life, were buried in the same grave.

When Massinger came to London, the English drama, as I have said, was at its height. But before he had begun any dramatic work of importance the turning-point had been reached, and the period of descent or degeneration begun. Elizabethan had given place to Stuart England, and with the dynasty the whole spirit of the nation was changing. Fletcher and Massinger together represent this period: Fletcher by painting with dashing brilliance the light, bright, showy, superficial aristocratic life of wild and graceful wantonness; Massinger by painting with a graver and a firmer brush, in darker colours and more considered outlines, the shadier side of the same impressive and unsatisfactory existence. The indications of lessening vitality and strength, of departing simplicity, of growing extravagance and affectation, which mark the period of transition, reappear in the drama of Massinger, as in that of Shirley, and sever it, by a wide and visible gulf, from the drama which we properly name Elizabethan. Massinger is the late twilight of the long and splendid day of which Marlowe was the dawn.

The characteristics of any poet's genius are seen clearly in his versification. Massinger's verse is facile, vigorous, grave, in the main correct; but without delicacy or rarity, without splendour or strength of melody; the verse of a man who can write easily, and who is not always too careful to remember that he is writing poetry. Owing, no doubt, partly to the facility with which he wrote, Massinger often has imperfectly accentuated lines, such as:

> They did expect to be chain'd to the oar.

Coleridge has remarked on the very slight degree in which Massinger's verse is distinguished from prose; and no one can read a page of any of his plays without being struck by it. It is not merely that a large proportion of the lines run on and overlap their neighbours; this is only the visible sign of a radical peculiarity. The pitch of Massinger's verse is somewhat lower than the proper pitch of poetry; somewhat too near the common pitch of prose. Shakespeare, indeed, in his latest period, extended the rhythm of verse to its loosest and freest limits; but not merely did he never pass beyond the invisible and unmistakeable boundary, he retained the true intonation of poetry as completely as in his straitest periods of metrical restraint.

Massinger set himself to follow in the steps of Shakespeare, and he succeeded in catching with admirable skill much of the easy flow and conversational facility at which he aimed. "His English style," says Lamb, "is the purest and most free from violent metaphors and harsh constructions, of any of the dramatists who were his contemporaries." But this "pure and free" style obtains its freedom and purity at a heavy cost; or let us say rather, the style possesses a certain degree of these two qualities because of the absence of certain others. Shakespeare's freest verse is the fullest of episodical beauties and of magical lines. But it is a singular thing, especially singular in a writer distinguished not only by fluency but by dignity and true eloquence, that in the whole of Massinger's extant works there are scarcely a dozen lines of intrinsic and separable beauty. It would be useless to look in the Massinger part of

The Virgin Martyr for any such lines as these of Dekker:

> I could weary stars,
> And force the wakeful moon to lose her eyes,
> By my late watching.

It would be equally useless to search from end to end of his plays. Easy flowing lines, vigorous lines, eloquent and persuasive lines, we could find in plenty; but nowhere a line in which colour melts into music, and both become magical. Not quite so difficult, but still very hard indeed, would it be to find any single lines of that rare and weighty sort which may be said to resemble the jar in the *Arabian Nights* into which Solomon had packed the genie. Had Massinger wished to represent Vittoria Accoramboni before her judges, he would have written for her a thoroughly eloquent, admirable, and telling oration; but he could never have wrought her speech into that dagger with which Webster drives home the sharpness of her imperial scorn. That one line of infinite meaning:

> Cover her face; mine eyes dazzle; she died young;

spoken by Ferdinand in *The Duchess of Malfy* over the corpse of his murdered sister, has no parallel in Massinger, who would probably have begun a long and elaborate piece of rhetoric with

> Stay, I feel
> A sudden alteration.

If we carry these considerations further, we shall see how fully the mental characteristics of Massinger correspond with the evidences of them in his versification. The ease and facility shown in the handling of metre are manifest equally in the plot and conduct of the plays. Massinger thoroughly understood the art of the playwright. No one perhaps, after Shakespeare, proved himself so constantly capable of constructing an orderly play and working it steadily out. His openings are as a rule admirable; thoroughly effective, explanatory and preparatory. How well, for instance, the first scene of *The Duke of Milan* prepares us, by a certain uneasiness or anxiety in its trembling pitch of happiness, for the events which are to follow! It is not always possible to say as much for his conclusions. Ingenuity, certainly, and considerable constructive skill, are there, in a greater or less degree; and in not a few instances (as in that delightful play *The Great Duke of Florence*, or in that powerful play *Believe as You List*) the conclusion is altogether right and satisfying. But in many instances Massinger's very endeavour to wind off his play in the neatest manner, without any tangles or frayed edges, spoils the proper artistic effect. His persistent aversion to a tragic end, even where a virtual tragedy demands it; his invincible determination to make things come to a fortunate conclusion, even if the action has to be huddled up or squashed together in consequence; in a word, his concession to the popular taste, no matter at what cost, not unfrequently distorts the conclusion of plays up to this point well conducted.

Massinger's treatment of character follows in some respects, while it seems in others to contradict, his treatment of versification and of construction. Where Massinger most conclusively fails is in a right understanding and a right representation of human nature; in the power to conceive passion and bring its speech and action vividly and accurately before us. His theory of human nature is apparently that of the puppet-player: he is aware of violent but not of consistent action, of change but not of development. No dramatist talks so much of virtue and vice, but he has no conception of either except in the abstract; and he finds it not in the least surprising that a virtuous woman should suddenly cry out:

> Chastity,
> Thou only art a name, and I renounce thee!

or that a fanatical Mohammedan should embrace Christianity on being told that the Prophet was a juggler, and taught birds to feed in his ear. His motto might be:

> We are all the balls of time, tossed to and fro;

for his conception of life is that of a game of wild and inconsequent haphazard. It is true that he rewards his good people and punishes the bad with the most scrupulous care; but the good or bad person at the end of a play is not always the good or bad person of the beginning. Massinger's outlook is by no means vague or sceptical on religion[1] or on morals; he is moralist before all things, and the copy-book tags neatly pinned on to the conclusion of each play are only a somewhat clumsy exhibition of a real conviction and conscientiousness. But his morality is nerveless, and aimless in its general effect; or it translates itself, oddly enough, into a co-partner of confusion, a disturbing and distracting element of mischief.

Notwithstanding all we may say of Massinger's facility, it is evident that we have in him no mere improvisator, or contentedly hasty and superficial person. He was an earnest thinker, a thoughtful politician, a careful observer of the manners and men of his time, and, to the extent of his capacity, an eager student of human nature; but, for all that, his position is that of a foreigner travelling through a country of whose language he knows but a few words or sentences. He observes with keenness, he infers with acumen; but when he proceeds to take the last step, the final touch which transmutes recorded observation into vital fact, he finds (or we, at least, find) that his strength is exhausted, his limit reached. He observes, for instance, that the characters and motives of men are in general mixed; and especially, and in a

[1] *The Renegado* is a treatise on Christian evidence, *The Virgin Martyr* a chronicle of Christian martyrdom, *The Maid of Honour* concludes with a taking of the veil.

special degree, those of men of a certain class, and in certain positions. But when we look at the personages whom he presents before us as mixed characters, we perceive that they are not so in themselves, but are mixed in the making. "We do not forbid an artist in fiction," says Mr. Swinburne in speaking of Charles Reade, "to set before us strange instances of inconsistency and eccentricity in conduct; but we do require of the artist that he should make us feel such aberrations to be as clearly inevitable as they are confessedly exceptional." Now this is just what Massinger does not do; it is just here that he comes short of success as a dramatic artist. In Calderon's figure, we see his men dancing to the rhythm of a music which we cannot hear: nothing is visible to us but the grotesque contortions and fantastic motions of the dancer.

Where Massinger fails is in the power of identifying himself with his characters, at least in their moments of profound passion or strenuous action. At his best (or let us say, to be scrupulous, at almost his best) he succeeds on the one hand in representing the gentler and secondary passions and emotions; on the other, in describing the action of the primary passions very accurately and admirably, but, as it were, in the third person, and from the outside. As Mr. Leslie Stephen says with reference to a fine speech of Sir Giles Overreach in *A New Way to Pay Old Debts*, "Read 'he' for 'I,' and 'his' for 'my,' and it is an admirable bit of denunciation of a character probably intended as a copy from real life." His characters seldom quite speak out; they have almost always about them a sort of rhetorical self-consciousness. The language of pure passion is unknown to them; they can only strive to counterfeit its dialect. In handling a situation of tragic passion, in developing a character subject to the shocks of an antagonistic Fate, Massinger manifests a singular lack of vital force, a singular failure in the realizing imagination. He mistakes extravagance for strength, eloquence for conviction, feverishness for vitality. Take, for instance, the jealousy of Theodosius in *The Emperor of the East*. His conduct and language are altogether unreasoning and unreasonable, the extravagances of a weak and unballasted nature, depicted by one who can only thus conceive of strong passions. His sudden and overmastering jealousy at sight of the apple given by Eudocia to Paulinus is without probability; and Eudocia's lie when charged with the gift is without reason. It is almost too cruel in this connection to think of Desdemona's handkerchief; of the admirable and inevitable logic of the means by which Othello's mind is not so much imbued with suspicion as convinced with certainty. "All this pother for an apple!" as some sensible person in the play observes. Again, in *The Fatal Dowry*, compare for a moment Malefort's careful bombast, which leaves us cold and incredulous before an impossible and uninteresting monster of wickedness, with the biting and flaming words of Francesco Cenci, before which we shudder as at the fiery breath of the pit. Almost all Massinger's villains, notwithstanding the fearful language which they are in the habit of employing, fail to convince us of their particular wickedness; most of his tried and triumphant heroes fail to convince us of their vitality of virtue. Massinger's conception of evil is surprisingly naïve: he is frightened, completely taken in, by the big words and blustering looks of these bold and wicked men. He paints them with an inky brush, he tells us how very wicked they are, and he sets them denouncing themselves and their wickedness with a beautiful tenderness of conscience. The blackness of evil and the contrasted whiteness of virtue are alike lost on us, and the good moral with them; for we are unable to believe in the existence of any such beings. It is the same with those exhibitions of tempted virtue of which Massinger is so fond. I do not allude now to cases of actual martyrdom or persecution, such as those of Dorothea or Antiochus; but to situations of a more complex nature, such as that of Mathias with Honoria, or Bertoldo with Aurelia, in which we are expected to see the soul's conflict between virtue enthroned and vice assailant. The fault is that of inadequate realization of the true bearing of the situation; inadequate representation of the conflict which is very properly assumed to be going on. Massinger is like a man who knows that the dial-hand of the clock will describe a certain circle, passing from point to point of significant figures; but instead of winding up the clock, and setting it going of itself, he can only move round the hand on the outside. To use another figure, his characters oscillate rather than advance, their conversions are without saving effect on their souls, their falls have no damnation. They are alike outside themselves, and they talk of "my lust," "my virtue," as of detached and portable conveniences.

When we drop to a lower level than that of pure tragedy, when we turn to characters who are grave, or mild, or melancholy, or unfortunate, rather than passionate, intense, and flexible, we find that Massinger is more in his element. "Grave and great-hearted," as Mr. Swinburne calls him, he could bring before us, with sympathetic skill, characters whose predominant bent is towards a melancholy and great-hearted gravity, a calm and eloquent dignity, a self-sacrificing nobility of service, or lofty endurance of inevitable wrong. Massinger's favourite play was *The Roman Actor*: "I ever held it," he says in his dedication, "the most perfect birth of my Minerva." It is impossible to say quite that; but it is certainly representative of some among the noble qualities of its writer, while it shows very clearly the defects of these qualities. What it represents is scarcely human nature; but actions and single passions painted for the halls of kings. A certain cold loftiness, noble indeed, but not attained without some freezing of vital heat, informs it. Paris, the actor, is rather a grave and stately shadow than a breathing man; but the idealization is nobly conceived; and both actor and tyrant, Paris and Domitian, are, in their way, impressive figures, made manifest, not concealed, in rhetorical prolusions really appropriate to their time and character. Another classical play, the less-known *Believe as You List*, contains a figure in which I think we have the very best work of which Massinger was capable. The character of the deposed and exiled King Antiochus has a true heroism and kingliness about it; his language, a passionate and haughty dignity. The quiet constancy, the undaunted and uncomplaining endurance of the utmost ills of Fate, which mark the character and the utterance of the Asian Emperor, raise the poetry of the play to a height but seldom attained by the pedestrian Pegasus of Massinger. As Antiochus is the most impressive of his heroes, so Flaminius is one of the most really human and consistent of his villains. The end of the play is natural, powerful, and significant beyond that of any other; so natural, powerful, and significant, that we may feel quite sure it was received with doubtful satisfaction by the audience above whose head and against whose taste the poet had for once chosen to write.

In one or two striking portraits (those for example of the ironical old courtier Eubulus in *The Picture*, the old soldier Archidamus in *The Bondman*, or the faithful friend Romont in *The Fatal Dowry*) Massinger has shown his appreciation of honest worth and sober fidelity, qualities not of a showy kind, the recognition and representation of which do him honour. In *The Bashful Lover* and *The Maid of Honour* he has represented with special sympathy two phases of reverential and modest love. Hortensio, of the former, is a sort of pale Quixote, a knight-errant a little crazed; very sincere, and a trifle given to uttering vague and useless professions of hyperbolical humility and devotion. There is a certain febrile nobleness, a showy chivalry, about him; but we are conscious of something " got up " and over-conscious in the exhibition. Adorni, the rejected lover in *The Maid of Honour*, is a truly noble and pathetic picture; altogether without the specious eloquence and petted despair of Hortensio, but thoroughly human and rationally self-sacrificing. His duet with Camiola at the close of the third act is one of the very finest scenes in Massinger's works: that passage where the woman he loves despatches him to the rescue of the man on whom her own heart is set. " You will do this? " she says; and he answers, " Faithfully, madam," and then to himself aside, " but not live long after." A touch of this sort is but too rare in Massinger.

PHILIP MASSINGER

While I am speaking of *The Maid of Honour*, let me refer to the character of Camiola herself: incomparably Massinger's finest portrait of a woman. Camiola ("that small but ravishing substance," as, with a rare and infrequent touch of delicate characterization, she is somewhere called) is notwithstanding a few flaws in her delineation, a thoroughly delightful and admirable creature; full of bright strength and noble constancy, of womanly heart and most manly spirit and wit. Her bearing in the scene, to a part of which I have alluded, is admirable throughout; not admirable alone, but exquisite, are her quick "Never think more then" to the servant; her outcry about the "petty sum" of the ransom; and especially the words of "perfect moan" which fall from her when she learns the hopeless estate of her lover, imprisoned by his enemy, abandoned by his King:

> Possible! pray you, stand off.
> If I do not mutter treason to myself,
> My heart will break; and yet I will not curse him;
> He is my King. The news you have delivered
> Makes me weary of your company; we'll salute
> When we meet next. I'll bring you to the door.
> Nay, pray you, no more compliments.

When she learns of the treachery of the lover for whom she has done so much, her wondering and sorrowful "O Bertoldo!" is worth a world of rhetoric. It is she who utters the most famous phrase in Massinger, the fearless indictment of the

Court doctrine of the divinity of kings. "With your leave," she says to the King of Sicily,

> With your leave, I must not kneel, sir,
> While I reply to this: but thus rise up
> In my defence, and tell you, as a man,
> *(Since, when you are unjust, the deity,*
> *Which you may challenge as a king, parts from you)*
> 'Twas never read in holy writ, or moral,
> That subjects on their loyalty were obliged
> To love their sovereign's vices.

Her speech in answer to Bertoldo's hollow protestations of penitence, the "Pray you, rise," is full of delicate tact and subtle beauty of spirit.

Unfortunately all Massinger's women are not of the stamp of Camiola. Lidia, indeed, in *The Great Duke of Florence*, is a good, sweet, modest girl; Cleora in *The Bondman* would like to be so; Bellisant in *The Parliament of Love* is a brilliant, dashing creature; Margaret in *A New Way to Pay Old Debts* is an emphatically nice, shrewd, pleasant woman; and Matilda in *The Bashful Lover* a commonplace, decent young person, without a thread or shade of distinction. But Massinger's general conception of women, and the greater number of his portraits of them, are alike debased and detestable. His bad women are incredible monsters of preposterous vice; his good women are brittle and tainted. They breathe the air of courts, and the air is poisoned. Themselves the vilest, they walk through a violent and unnaturally vicious world of depraved imagination, greedy of pleasure and rhetorical of desire. They are shamefacedly shameless; offensive and without passion; importunate and insatiable Potiphar's wives. "Pleasure's their heaven," affirms somebody; and their pleasure is without bit or bridle, without rule or direction. Massinger's favourite situation is that of a queen or princess violently and heedlessly enamoured of a man, apparently of mean estate, though he generally turns out to be a duke in disguise, whom she has never seen five minutes before. Over and over again is this wretched farce gone through; always without passion, sincerity, or strength; always flatly, coldly, ridiculously. I am afraid Massinger thought his Donusas, Corsicas, Domitias, Aurelias, Honorias, and Beaumelles brilliant and fascinating flowers of evil, sisters of Cleopatra and Semiramis, magnificently wicked women. In reality they never attain to the level of a Delilah. They are vulgar-minded to the core; weak and without stability; mere animals if they are not mere puppets. The stain of sensuality or the smutch of vulgarity is upon even the virtuous. Marcelia, in *The Duke of Milan*, supposed to be a woman of spotless virtue, utters language full of covert licence; for Massinger seems to see virtue in women mainly as a sort of conscious and painful restraint. Eudocia, in *The Emperor of the East*, an injured, innocent wife, betrays an unconscious vulgarity of mind which is enough to withdraw our sympathy from a fairly well-deserving object. The curious thing is, not so much that the same pen could draw Camiola and Corsica, but that the same pen could draw Camiola and Marcelia.

Massinger's main field is the romantic drama. He attempted, indeed, tragedy, comedy, and history; but both tragedy and history assume in his hands a romantic cast, while his two great comedies verge constantly upon tragedy. Of his two most distinct and most distinguished tragedies, *The Duke of Milan* and *The Fatal Dowry*, the former is a powerful and impressive work, rising in parts to his highest level; the latter, despite its conventional reputation, which it owes partly to Rowe's effective plagiarization in *The Fair Penitent*, a scarcely adequate or satisfactory production. Two or three passages[1] in the latter part of *The Fatal Dowry* have the true accent of nature; but even these are marred by the base alloy with which they are mingled. But *The Duke of Milan*, despite much that is inadequate and even absurd in its handling, rises again and again to something of passion and of insight. The character and the circumstances of Sforza have been often compared with those of Othello: they are still more similar, I should venture to think, to those of Griffith Gaunt; and they have the damning fault of the latter, that the

---

[1] Found chiefly in the last scene of the fourth act; from "If this be to me, rise," to "That to be merciful should be a sin," and again in the few words following on the death of Beaumelle; with a passage or two in the fifth act.

PHILIP MASSINGER

jealousy and its consequences are not made to seem quite inevitable. Sforza is an example, though perhaps the most favourable one, of that inconsequential oscillation of nature to which I have already referred as characteristic of most of Massinger's prominent characters. But his capacity for sudden and extreme changes of disposition, and his violent and unhinged passion, are represented with more dramatic power, with more force and naturalness, than it is at all usual to find in Massinger; who has here contrived to give a frequent effect of fineness to the frenzies and delusions of his hero. If Sforza is after all but a second-rate Othello, Marcelia is certainly a very shrewish Desdemona, and Francisco a palpably poor Iago.[1]

In tragi-comedy, the romantic drama pure and simple, we may take *The Great Duke of Florence* as the most exquisite example. In this, the most purely delightful play, I think, ever written by Massinger, a play which we read, to use Lamb's expression, "with composure and placid delight," we see the sweetest and most delicate side of Massinger's genius: a country pleasantness and freshness, a masquerading and genial gravity, altogether charming and attractive. The plot is admirably woven; and how prettily brought about

---

[1] There is one touch, however, in the temptings of Francisco which is really almost worthy of Iago:
> She's yet guilty
> *Only* in her intent!

to a happy conclusion, with its good humour, forgiveness, and friendship all round! There is something almost of Shakespeare's charm in people and events; in these princes and courtiers without ceremony and without vice, uttering pretty sentiments prettily, and playing elegantly at life; in these simple lovers, with their dainty, easy trials and crosses on the way to happiness; in the villain who does no real harm, and whom nobody can hate. *The Guardian*, a late play, very fine and flexible in its rhythm, and very brisk in its action, has some exquisite country feeling, together with three or four of the most abominable characters and much of the vilest language in Massinger. One character at least, Darazzo, the male of Juliet's nurse, is really, though offensive enough in all conscience, very heartily and graphically depicted. *A Very Woman*, again, by Massinger and Fletcher,[1] has much that is pleasant and delightful; some of it full of sweetness, with some that is rank enough. I have spoken already of *The Maid of Honour*, or it might be mentioned here as a play uniting (somewhat as in *Measure for Measure*, which it partly resembles) the lighter and graver qualities of tragedy and comedy under the form of the romantic drama.

Massinger's lack of humour did not prevent him from writing comedy, nor yet from achieving signal

---

[1] Fletcher's slave-market scene in Act III is a piece of admirable merriment; singularly realistic and inventive.

success in it. *A New Way to Pay Old Debts* is the most memorable of his plays; but, though it is styled a comedy, it is certainly not for laughter that we turn to it. *A New Way* and *The City Madam* belong to the Comedy of Manners; satirical transcripts of contemporary life, somewhat after the style of Terence or Plautus. All Massinger's plays are distinguished by an earnest and corrective tone on contemporary politics and current fashions; and it is no wonder that he succeeded in a species of play devoted wholly to the exhibition and satirization of the follies and vanities of the day. His constant touch on manners, even in romantic plays with classical or eastern localities, is peculiar, and suggests a certain pre-occupation with the subject, possibly due to early associations at Wilton House, possibly to mere personal bent or circumstances. Remembering the letter of 1624, we may be allowed to fancy a personal applicability in the frequent denunciations of usurers and delineations of the misery of poor debtors. But besides this, I think that Massinger, having no force to enter into the deep and secret chambers of the soul, found his place to be in a censorship of society, and was right in concerning himself with what he could do so well. His professedly comic types, even Justice Greedy, are mere exaggerations, solitary traits frozen into the semblance of men, without really comic effect. But in the conduct of these two plays, in the episodical illuminations of London and provincial life, in the wealth of observation and satire which they exhibit, Massinger has left us work of permanent value; and in the character of Sir Giles Overreach he has made his single contribution to the gallery of permanent illustrations of human nature: a portrait to be spoken of with Grandet and with Harpagon.

Massinger is the product of his period, and he reflects faithfully the temper of court and society under the first Charles. Much that we have to regret in him was due to the misfortune of his coming just when he did, at the ebb of a spent wave; but the best that he had was all his own. Serious, a thinker, a moralist, gifted with an instinct for nobility and a sympathy in whatever is generous and self-sacrificing, a practical student of history, and an honest satirist of social abuses, he was at the same time an admirable story-teller, and a master of dramatic construction. But his grave and varied genius was lacking in the primary requirements of the dramatist: in imagination, in strength, in sincerity. He has no real mastery over the passions, and his eloquence does not appeal to the heart. He interests us strongly; but he does not convince us in spite of ourselves. The whole man is seen in the portrait by which we know him: in the contrast and contradiction of that singular face, which interests, to some degree attracts, yet never satisfies us, with its melancholy and thoughtful grace, marred by a certain vague weakness and a scarcely definable sense of something lacking.

JOHN DAY

"JOHN DAY, sometime student of Caius College, Cambridge," a "base fellow" and a "rogue" according to Ben Jonson, a good man and a charming writer if the evidence of his own plays may be credited, seems to have come down to posterity in the person of his best work, and of little beside his best. When he began to write for the stage is not known (before 1593, some have supposed) but we learn from Henslowe's Diary that, in the six years from 1598 to 1603, he had a whole or part share in as many as twenty-two plays, only one of which, *The Blind Beggar of Bednal Green*, has come down to us. These plays were: in 1598, *The Conquest of Brute, with the first finding of the Bath* (Day, assisted by Chettle); in 1599, *The Tragedy of Merry* and *The Tragedy of Cox of Collumpton* (with Haughton), *The Orphan's Tragedy* (with Haughton and Chettle); in 1600, unassisted, *The Italian Tragedy of* . . . . (name wanting in the Diary), *The Spanish Moor's Tragedy* and *The Seven Wise Masters* (with Dekker and Haughton), *The Golden Ass*, and *Cupid and Psyche* (with Dekker and Chettle), *The Blind Beggar of Bednal Green* (with Chettle); in 1601, *The Second Part of the Blind Beggar*, and *The Third Part* (also with Chettle), *The Conquest of the West Indies* (with Haughton and Wentworth Smith), *The Six Yeoman of the West, Friar Rush and the Proud Woman of Antwerp,* and *The Second Tart of Tom Dough* (all three with Haughton); in 1602, unassisted, *The Bristol Tragedy, Merry as may be, The Black Dog of Newgate, The Second Part of the Black Dog, The Unfortunate General* (all with Hathway and Wentworth Smith), and *The Toast of Billingsgate* (with Hathway and others); in 1603, or earlier, *Jane Shore* (with Chettle). In 1610, we learn from the Stationers' Register, Day wrote a play called *The Mad Pranks of Merry Moll of the Bankside*; in 1619, with Dekker, *The Life and Death of Guy of Warwick*; again with Dekker, in or before 1623, a "French tragedy" of *The Bellman of Paris;* and in 1623, a comedy, *Come, see a Wonder.* Of extant plays, *The Isle of Gulls* was published in 1606; *The Travels of the Three English Brothers, Sir Thomas, Sir Anthony, Mr. Robert Shirley* (written in conjunction with Rowley and Wilkins), in 1607; *Law-Tricks, or Who would have thought it,* and *Humour out of Breath,* in 1608; *The Parliament of Bees,* in 1641; and *The Blind Beggar* in 1659. There is also extant in the British Museum (Sloane MS. 3150) an allegorical prose tract entitled *Peregrinatio Scholastica,* first published in Mr. Bullen's collected edition of Day's works in 1881; a begging acrostic on the name of Thomas Dowton, an actor; an undated letter of Day from which we learn of a poem on *The Miracles of Christ*; a few lines in his handwriting, belonging to some lost historical play: "the rest is silence."

It is not a pleasant thought that a writer of such dainty and select genius as the author of *The Parliament of Bees* should have had to labour so hard on such unworthy material, for so unthankworthy a public as that which left him to borrow of Henslowe two shillings, or it may be five shillings, "in redy money," as the record quaintly states. That the main part at least of these lost plays was but journeyman's work, work sufficient to the day and the evil thereof, seems evident from the mere titles, a small proportion, no doubt, of the whole, that have come down to us. Even Mr. Bullen finds it impossible to regret the loss, and he would be content to spare *The Three English Brothers* and *The Blind Beggar* as well. The fact is, Day's range is exceptionally limited, and outside his circle he has no magic.

In turning over the pages of Lamb's *Specimens*, it is with something of relief, after so much of blood and shadow, that we come on the two or three brief extracts from *The Parliament of Bees*, by which alone, for so long a space of time, the name of John Day was known to English readers. They are so light and bright, so delicate in the wording and phrasing, so aloof and apart from the commonness of everyday doings, or the sombre action of that little world of the Elizabethan drama. The choicest of Day's work comes with just such a sense of relief to the student who has traversed that country widely. It is a wayside rest, a noonday hour in the cool shadow of the woods. There is something so pleasant about the work, that we find ourselves pardoning, almost without thinking about them, faults and shortcomings which in another would have caused us an instinctive irritation. Day, it is clear if we think carefully about it, has but a very slight insight into human nature, only a very faint power of touching or moving us, no power whatever to mould a coherent figure or paint a full-length portrait; as for plot, he is content with none at all, as in the *Bees*, or, as in the other three comedies, with a plot of such fantastic and intricate slightness, a very spider's-web of filmy threads, that it is not to be grasped without coming to pieces. His wit is a clear flame, but only thin and faint; and it is only intermittent. Day's natural wealth in that way is not so rich that it can stand a long draw on its exchequer. The good money becomes used up, and then, instead of putting up the shutters, the bank passes bad currency. All these are serious faults; they are leaks enough to sink a weightier reputation; but somehow they do no more than temper our delight in Day. The world of his fancy is not the world of our common sunlight; and life is lived otherwise, and men and women are somewhat other, than the men and women who cast no shadows as they walk there. It is a land into which the laws of reason can scarcely come; a land where gentle and petulant figures come and go like figures in a masque, aimlessly enough, yet to measure, always with happy effect, threading the forest paths as we see ourselves in sleeping or waking dreams, ever on the heels of some pleasing or exciting adventure. The conversation, where it is good, is carried on in jests, or in flights of lyrical fancy, somewhat as in Shakespeare's early comedies, somewhat with a sort of foretaste of the comedies of Congreve. If it is not the talk of real life, it is at least a select rendering of our talk at its freest, when the brain is quickened and the tongue loosened by some happy chance, among responsive friends in tune with a blithe mood. It is how we should often like to talk; and that accord with our likings of things, as apart from our consciousness, not always pleasant, of them, is the secret of a certain harmony we seem to feel in those parts of Day's comedies which are least like life. He steps quite through the ugly surface of things, freeing us, as we take the step with him, of all the disabilities of our never quite satisfied existence.

This land of fancy to which Day leads us is essentially quite as much a land of fancy in the comedies which profess to chronicle the doings of men and women, as in the comedy whose characters are bees. In *The Isle of Gulls, Law-Tricks,* and *Humour out of Breath,* equally as to the spirit of them, very differently as regards the point of execution, Day has painted life as it pleased him to see it: in a delightful confusion, made up of entanglements, disguises, jests, sudden adventures, good-hearted merriment, a comedy within a comedy. Compared with *Humour out of Breath,* the two other plays have a certain coarseness of texture; the action is not so pleasant, nor the wit so spontaneous. They are immensely lively, always entertaining, ravelled up with incomparable agility, full of business, wit, and humour; breaking every now and then into seriousness, and, in the later play particularly, blossoming out quite unexpectedly into a tender and lyrical pathos; as in that scene where the forsaken countess talks with a gentle sadness to her maids as they sit at their sewing; a little passage of pure charm, reminding one, as now and again Day will remind us, of certain of the most purely charming passages of Shakespeare. In another single scene in *The Isle of Gulls,* the Tennis-court scene, we find a quite typical example of Day's special variety of wit, thin and captious indeed, but swift in its interchange of strokes as the very tennis-balls, flying to and fro, with sharp and harmless knocks, in repartees deftly delivered and straight to their aim. It is in *Humour out of Breath,* however, so suggestively named, and so truly, for the little play keeps us breathless at the heels of its breathless actors, here, rather than anywhere else outside *The Parliament of Bees*, that the special note of Day's cheerful genius is heard most clearly. It has his finest polish, the cream of his wit, the pick of his women. Day's women are singularly charming: they are all of one type, and that no very subtle one, but they are immensely likeable, and the most likeable of them all is in this play, Florimel, Emilia's sister, Hippolyta's and Violetta's, but the most beautiful and brilliant of her sisters. Emilia in *Law-Tricks* reminds us, by anticipation, of Millimant, as Miso in *The Isle of Gulls*, with her "As I am a Lady," seems almost like a faint foreshadowing of the most tragic figure on the English comic stage, Lady Wishfort. But Florimel, calling up no associations of Congreve or any other, proves the most delightful of companions. She, like her sisters, is a creature of moods, bright, witty, full of high spirits, very free spoken, but less free in action than in speech: you can see her lips and eyes in a smile, flashing as her saucy words; and she is good-hearted, capable of strength in love; a thoroughly English girl. Here, as so often elsewhere, we cannot but note Day's instinctive sympathy with whatsoever is honest, lovely, and of good report. He cannot conceive a villain; his fantastic figures and the fantasy of his action have alike a basis of honesty and rectitude. Just this quality, going out into very homely material, gives to the hasty, irregular, romping play of *The Blind Beggar of Bednal Green* a saving grace, not of morals, but of art; for it is a touch of nature. Touches of nature there are, but of another kind, in *Humour out of Breath*; always, however sincere, however serious, with an after-thought or atmosphere of brightness in or about them: as in Aspero's wooing of Florimel, passing out of jests and quibbles into hearty earnest; earnest from the first perhaps on both sides, though the lady has a dancing wit, and the gentleman goads a sober tongue to curvets. How pretty a touch of nature is this: " I cannot live without him!" cries Florimel, when her saucy petulance has driven away her lover. " O that he knew it, lady!" suggests the quick-witted little page, at fault for once in a lover's moods; for, " He does," returns Florimel, never at fault; "he would never have left me else. He does!" Touches of this sort, true to nature in the more intimate and subtle sense, are not common in Day; he does not often reveal anything new to us in our own hearts. It would be unfair to lay this to his charge, for he does not profess to give us more than we find in him. " Humour out of breath," a world where wit is the atmosphere of life, this is what he gives us; a world (how delightful to contemplate!) where men and women are so careful of their jests, and of the measure and harmony of this absorbing business of play, that they will even (as Polymeter says on some occasion, elsewhere) "leave at a jest," and turn the conversation after a period of punning.

I have said that the scene of these three comedies is virtually a land of fancy; in *The Parliament of Bees* it is not only virtually, but formally so. No instinct could have been happier than that which led Day (could it have been with any thought of Aristophanes?) to turn the "men and women fashioned by his fancy" into bees, and give them a whole play to themselves. That this was an afterthought, only come upon after a large part of what now forms the play was written, seems evident; for, as Mr. Bullen has pointed out, "with the exception of characters 1, 11, and 12, which were plainly written for the occasion, the masque seems to have been made up of scenes, more or less revised, contributed to (Dekker's) *Wonder of a Kingdom* (Samuel Rowley's) *Spanish Soldier*, and other plays that have either been lost or where the connection remains yet to be pointed out." There is not even an attempt at anything like a plot; what we have is a sequence of scenes, sketching, and lightly satirizing, the "humours" of the age under this queer disguise of the bees. It is doubtful whether Day ever intended it, but in this fantastic masque of his there are all the elements of an heroically comic picture of life; life seen from the point of view of an outside observer, in all its eager stir and passion, its strenuous littleness, its frail strength, its gigantic self-delusions, so petty and so vain if one could look down upon it; as petty and vain, to the eternal spectator of things, as these tiny creatures, with their insect life of a summer, seem to men. Here is the quack, the braggart, the spendthrift, each with all the passions of a man: and just as long as your nail! But if this view enters at all into Day's scheme, it is permitted to add no bitterness, no touch of spleen, to this sweet and gracious little play, revised, as we know from an earlier manuscript still existing, with such a tender care, not only for the clear polish of the lines, but equally for the pleasant wholesomeness of the story, the honesty and fair fame of the personages. Quite the best scene, the sixth, between Arethusa and Ulania concerning Meletus, has gained the most from this revision: it is free now from any speck, and is one of the loveliest pastorals in our language, a little masterpiece of dainty invention, honey-hearted and without a sting; touching at one point, in the last speech of the poor neglected bee, the ultimate limits of Day's capacity for pensive and tender pathos. Nothing in the play is so beelike, nothing so human, as this all-golden episode; though in pastoral beauty it is touched, I think, by the wood-notes of the final octosyllabics; verses of exquisite inappropriateness for bees, but with all the smell and freshness of the country in them, a pageant of the delightful things of nature and husbandry, written in rhymes that seem to gambol two and two, like lambs in spring.

Without *The Parliament of Bees* we should never have known what Day was capable of. The wit and invention of his comedies of adventure make up, it is true, a very distinct and a very important part of his claim on the attention of posterity; but these comedies, after all, are very largely written, especially in the best parts of them, in prose, and it is as a poetical craftsman that Day is most himself and most perfect. Such a line as this:

Who then shall reap the golden crop you sow?

bears the very sign and seal of Day. Or, again:

The windows of my hive, with blossoms dight,
Are porters to let in our comfort, light.

Our comfort, light: the very cadence of these beautiful words rings of Day, and the meaning equally with the sound. His peculiar vein of fancy comes out typically in those lines where the Plush Bee longs, like Alexander, for "ten worlds," indeed to sell, but to sell *"for Alpine hills of silver."* Familiar and quite ordinary ideas, commonplace thoughts, take in his mind an aspect which gives them all the charm of a pleasing novelty, a fanciful aspect, the good cheer of fancy. There is often an airy spring in his moods, lifting his honest commonplaces quite off the ground; transforming them, as frost transforms and transfigures the bare branches of the trees. The very sound of his rhymes is a delight in itself, as in those lines which tell how

> of the sudden, listening, you shall hear
> A noise of horns and hunting, which shall bring
> Actæon to Diana in the spring.

Instinctive harmony, a sense of delicate music in the fall and arrangement of quite common words, this is his gift, and it is apparently without effort that verse flows after verse with this elegance of cadence, so easy does it seem for him to "add to golden numbers golden numbers." Easy or not, we know it was not without labour that this play became what it is. Day was no trifler, slight, airy, fantastically delicate as his work may be; it was not a trifler, a workman careless of the things of art, who wrote these lines:

> The true Poet indeed doth scorn to gild
> A coward's tomb with glories, or to build
> A sumptuous pyramid of golden verse
> Over the ruins of an ignoble hearse.
> *His lines like his invention are born free,*
> *And both live blameless to eternity:*
> He holds his reputation so dear
> As neither flattering hope nor servile fear
> Can bribe his pen to temporize with kings:
> The blacker are their crimes, he louder sings.

The writer of these splendid lines was no "base fellow," as Ben Jonson said in his haste, but a poet with an instinctive sense of melody which Jonson never possessed, and an ideal of art as lofty as Jonson's own. His work has no conquering force, no massive energy, no superabundance of life; these qualities we can get elsewhere, but nowhere save in Day that special charm of fancy and wit and bright invention, "golden murmurs from a golden hive," for which it is pleasant to suppose his name will live yet a little longer.

II. STUDIES IN CONTEMPORARY LITERATURE

CHRISTINA ROSSETTI

By the death of Christina Rossetti, literature, and not English literature alone, has lost the one great modern poetess. There is another English poetess, indeed, who has gained a wider fame; but the fame of Mrs. Browning, like that of her contemporary, and, one might almost say, companion, George Sand, was of too immediate and temporary a kind to last. The very feminine, very emotional, work of Mrs. Browning, which was really, if we look into it closely, but little more than literature of the L. E. L. order carried to its furthest limits, roused a sort of womanly enthusiasm, in precisely the same way as the equally feminine, equally emotional, work of George Sand. In the same way, but in a lesser degree, all the women who have written charming verse (and how many there have been in quite recent times!) have won, and deservedly, a certain reputation as poetesses among poetesses. In Miss Rossetti we have a poet among poets, and in Miss Rossetti alone. Content to be merely a woman, wise in limiting herself within somewhat narrow bounds, she possessed, in union with a profoundly emotional nature, a power of artistic self-restraint which no other woman who has written in verse, except the supreme Sappho, has ever shown; and it is through this mastery over her own nature, this economy of her own resources, that she takes rank among poets rather than among poetesses.

And, indeed, the first quality that appeals to one in Miss Rossetti's work is its artistic finish; and this finish is apparent in a simplicity so intense, so expressive, and so casual in seeming, as only the finest elaboration could extract from the complexities and confusions of nature. Her preference was for the homeliest words, and for the rhythms in which the art consists in a seeming disregard of art. No one who ever wrote in verse used so many words of one syllable, or so few words not used in ordinary conversation. No one ever used fewer inversions, or was less dependent on the unusual in sound or colour, or found less need or less room for metaphor. Italian as she partly was, there is absolutely nothing in her of the Italian luxuriance in language, that luxuriance which flowered so strangely in the poetry of her brother. She is more English than any Englishwoman. And yet, with these plain, unadorned words, the words that come first to our lips when we speak to one another, she obtained effects, not merely of vivid sincerity, of downright passion, of religious conviction, but also of fantastic subtlety, of airy grace, of remote and curious charm. Fairyland to her was as real as it is to a child, and it is with all a child's quaint familiarity with the impossible that she sings of "Goblin Market." It is with something also of the child's terror and attraction that she tells of ghosts, of dead people, buried and unhappy in their graves, who try vainly, or perhaps not quite in vain, to get back into the warmth and strangeness of life. And the genuine shiver which she strikes through us is certainly a tribute to what is so deceptively matter-of-fact in her way of dealing with the mysterious. Just so the familiar and modest confidence with which she approaches what is rare and subtle in its beauty, as if at home there, awakens in us the sense of rarity and beauty, as a more oppressed and anxious air of attendance on the great in state fails, often enough, to do. We hear the music of her verse afloat in the air, the very music of Ariel, and yet with all the intimacy of a perfume, the perfume of a flower; the soul of something living and beautiful, with its roots in the earth.

This felicitously simple art, in which style is never a separate grace, but part of the very texture, so to speak, of the design, is the expression of a nature in which intensity of feeling is united with an almost painful reserve. It is as if the writer were forced, in spite of her utmost endeavour, to give voice to certain deep emotions, the cry of the heart for love, the soul's cry to God. The words seem as if wrung out of her, and it is in their intense quietness that one realizes the controlling force of the will that has bound them down. Alike in the love poems and in the religious poems, there is a certain asceticism, passion itself speaking a chastened language, the language, generally, of sorrowful but absolute renunciation. This motive, passion remembered and repressed, condemned to eternal memory and eternal sorrow, is the motive of much of her finest work; of "The Convent Threshold," for instance, that "masterpiece of ascetic passion," as Dante Rossetti called it. Its recurrence gives a certain sadness to her verse, in spite of so much that is quaint, playful, and childlike in it. The finest of her earlier poems was a paraphrase on Ecclesiastes, and the vanity, shortness, and broken happiness of life are ever present to her. She utters no unseemly complaint, she brings no accusation against Providence, but she has no illusions in regard to things. And in her religious poems, which are perhaps the finest part of her work in verse, it is with a mainly tragic ecstasy that she sends up her soul to God, out of the depths. She is not less conscious of human unworthiness than of the infinite charity of God; and in her passionate humility she prays for the lowest place in Paradise, finding "that lowest place too high." Hers is, indeed, a rapture, but contained, constrained, saddened with a conscious unworthiness, grave with the sorrow of the world. It is not the soaring rapture of a Crashaw, which shrieks aloud, almost, in the fever of its devotional ecstasy; much less is it akin to the dusty, daily pieties of George Herbert. Less delirious than Crashaw, less composed than George Herbert, Miss Rossetti takes her place as a religious poet between the one and the other, and she takes that place on terms of equality. Even in the little edifying books which she wrote with the deliberate intention of doing good, there is a firm and assured art in the handling of the very difficult matter of devotion. With her, the service of God, to which, in her later years, she gave herself with an absolute retirement from all worldly interests and undertakings, was hieratic in its solemnity, and demanded all the myrrh and frankincense and gold of art, as but an honourable return of gifts in homage to the giver. Here, as in the love-poems, depth of feeling is made no excuse for laxity of form; but the form is ennobled, and chastened into a finer severity, in proportion to the richness of the sentiment which it enshrines. It is by this rare, last quality of excellence, that Christina Rossetti takes her place among the great poets of our century, not on sufferance, as a woman, but by right, as an artist.

A power of seeing finely beyond the scope of ordinary vision; that, in a few words, is the note of Miss Rossetti's genius, and it brings with it a subtle and as if instinctive power of expressing subtle and yet as if instinctive conceptions; always clearly, always simply, with a singular and often startling homeliness, which is the sincerity of a style that seems to be innocently unaware of its own beauty. This power is shown in every division of her poetry; in the peculiar witchery of the poems dealing with the supernatural, in the exaltation of the poems of devotion, in the lyrical quality of the songs of children, birds, and corn, in the special variety and the special excellence of the poems of passion and meditation. The union of homely yet always select literalness of treatment with mystical visionariness, or visionariness which is sometimes mystical, constitutes the peculiar quality of her poetry; poetry which seems to divide itself into several natural divisions.

Miss Rossetti's power of seeing what others do not see, and of telling us about it in such a way that we too are able to see it, is displayed nowhere more prominently than in those poems which deal, in one way or another, with the supernatural. A sense of the mystery enveloping our life, a "vague spiritual fear" and curiosity, is, strangely enough, the common possession of the least and the most imaginative persons. We see it equally in the half-animal terror of the ploughboy crossing the graveyard hurriedly by night, and in the nervous ecstasy of Hoffmann before the spectres of his own creation. In both these extremes there is something painful, bewildering, a sensation as of perilous insecurity. But children, who are capable of deriving intense agony from the thought of the supernatural, feel also an intense delight in certain happy and fantastic aspects of it, and have a singular power of realizing the scenes and the inhabitants of that mid-region of the unseen world which we call Fairyland. In one poem of Miss Rossetti's we find the most perfect expression ever given to this milder aspect of the supernatural. "Goblin Market" is surely the most naïve and childlike poem in our language. Miss Rossetti's witchcraft is so subtle that she seems to bewitch, not only us, but herself, and without trying to do either. The narrative has so matter-of-fact, and at the same time so fantastic and bewildering an air, that we are fairly puzzled into acceptance of everything. The very rhythm, the leaping and hopping rhythm, which renders the goblin merchantmen visible to us, has something elfin, and proper to "the little people," in its almost infantile jingle and cadence. In "The Prince's Progress" we are in quite another corner of the world of faëry. The poem is more mature, it is handled in a more even and masterly way; but it is, after all, more like other romantic ballads (William Morris's, for instance) than "Goblin Market" is like anything at all. The narrative is in the purely romantic manner, and the touch of magic comes into it suddenly and unawares, like the green glitter that comes into the eyes of the milkmaid as she casts her glamour over the Prince on the way. The verse is throughout flexible and expressive, but towards the end, just before and during the exquisite lament, bride-song and death-song at once, it falls into a cadence of such solemn and tender sweetness as even Miss Rossetti has rarely equalled.

Yet another phase of the supernatural meets us in a little group of poems ("The Ghost's Petition," "The Hour and the Ghost," "At Home," "The Poor Ghost") in which the problems of the unseen world are dealt with in a singular way. Miss Rossetti's genius is essentially sombre, or it writes itself at least on a dark background of gloom. The thought of death has a constant fascination for her, almost such a fascination as it had for Leopardi or Baudelaire; only it is not the fascination of attraction, as with the one, nor of repulsion, as with the other, but of interest, sad but scarcely unquiet interest in what the dead are doing underground, in their memories, if memory they have, of the world they have left; a singular, whimsical sympathy with the poor dead, like that expressed in two famous lines of the *Fleurs du Mal*.

These strange little poems, with their sombre and fantastic colouring, the picturesque outcome of a deep and curious pondering over unseen things, lead easily, by an obvious transition, to the poems of spiritual life, in the customary or religious sense of the term. Miss Rossetti's devotional poetry is quite unlike most other poetry of the devotional sort. It is intensely devout, sometimes almost liturgical in character; surcharged with personal emotion, a cry of the heart, an ecstasy of the soul's grief or joy: never didactic, or concerned with purposes of edification. She does not preach; she prays. We are allowed to overhear a dialogue of the soul with God. Her intensity of religious feeling touches almost on the ecstasy of Jacopone da Todi, but without his delirium. In such a poem as "Despised and Rejected," in which Christ stands at the door and knocks, at the unopening door of the heart, the reality of the externalised emotion is almost awful; it is scarcely to be read without a shudder. In "Advent," another masterpiece, the ecstasy is of faith, faith triumphant after watching and waiting, after vigils and darkness: a cry from spiritual watch-towers. In all these poems we are led through phase after phase of a devout soul; we find a sequence of keen and brooding moods of religious feeling and meditation; with, in the less sombre pieces, a sort of noting of the sensations of the soul; with, also, something of the ingenious quaintness, the solemn curiosity of Donne, allied to something of the instinctive and unaccountable felicity of Shelley.

In Miss Rossetti's religious poems there is a recurring burden of lament over the vanity of things, the swiftness of the way to death, the faithlessness of affection, the relentless pressure of years, finding voice in the magnificent paraphrase on Ecclesiastes (the early poem called "A Testimony") in the two splendid sonnets, "Vanity of Vanities," and "One

Certainty," and, less sadly, in the little lyric masterpiece, " Passing away, saith the World, passing away!" "Vanity of Vanities" is what she sees written upon all beautiful and desirable things; a great shadow or cloud over life, a ceaseless reminder of the sure end and the great change. I have spoken of her strange curiosity about the future, about what comes after death; she can also, like Keats, be "half in love with easeful death;" and in such a mood she can sing of nothing with so delicate a desire and sympathy as the narrow grave that is to cover us in at last.

> Underneath the growing grass,
>   Underneath the living flowers,
>   Deeper than the sound of showers:
>   There we shall not count the hours
> By the shadows as they pass.
>
> Youth and health will be but vain,
>   Beauty reckoned of no worth:
>   There a very little girth
>   Can hold round what once the earth
> Seemed too narrow to contain.

That is how she sings of " The Bourne." But the quiet sadness of these poems of abstract meditation over the vanity of things, passes, when we turn to another well-defined class of poems, into a keener and more personal sorrow. There is one subject to which Miss Rossetti returns again and again, a subject into which she is able to infuse a more intense feeling than we find in any but her devotional pieces: that of a heart given sorrowfully over to the memory of a passion spent somehow in vain, disregarded or self-repressed. In such poems as that named "Twice," she has found singularly moving words for the suppressed bitterness of a disappointed heart, the anguish of unuttered passion reaching to a point of ascetic abnegation, a devout frenzy of patience, which is the springing of the bitter seed of hope dead in a fiery martyrdom. It is in "The Convent Threshold" that this conception obtains its finest realization. Passion, imagination, the romantic feeling, the religious fervour, the personal emotion, all her noblest gifts and qualities, with her noblest possibilities of style and versification, meet here as one. In this poem the passion is almost fierce. In "Monna Innominata: a Sonnet of Sonnets," the masterpiece of a later volume, a much quieter, perhaps only a sadder, voice is given to the same cry of an unsatisfied and unweariable love, the love of an "unnamed lady" for one between herself and whom there is a barrier, "held sacred by both, yet not such as to render mutual love incompatible with mutual honour:" self-repression and self-abnegation keep down its heart, a dignified prisoner behind very real bars. This sonnet-sequence should and will take its place among the great works of that kind, if delicate art, perfect within its limits, wedded to delicately sincere and deep emotion, limited, too, within a certain range, can give it right of admission among the stronger and more varied sequences of Dante and Petrarch, of Mrs. Browning and Rossetti.

In a world which wears chiefly an aspect of gloom for her, which is tragical in its earnestness, when it is not tragical in its pain or passion, there are still for Miss Rossetti, as for all sane and healthy spirits in however dark a world, two elements of pure joy, two eternal comforters: nature and children. There are poets who have attempted to read into nature, when they turned away from their own hearts, all the trouble and disquietude, the passion and hope and disaster, of human existence. Narcissus gazing into the water, and seeing only his own face looking back into himself, a worn and wearied face from which he cannot get free; this, so nearly the type of Dante Rossetti, is far from being the type of his sister. To her, nature is always a relief, an escape; certain aspects she responds to with a peculiarly exhilarating joyousness. It is always the calm aspects of natural things, and chiefly growing nature, that waken sympathy and delight in her. What we call scenery she never refers to; nor to mountains, nor often to the sea. But nowhere in poetry can we get such lovingly minute little pictures of flowers, and corn, and birds, and animals; of the seasons, particularly of spring. She delights in just such things as are the delight of a child; her observation is, as of set purpose, very usually that of a thoughtful and observant child. Children, we must remember, especially very small children, play a great part in the world of Miss Rossetti's poetry. They have, indeed, a book all to themselves, one of the quaintest and prettiest books in the language. *Sing-song: a Nursery Rhymebook*, illustrated with pictures, almost equal to the poems, by Arthur Hughes, makes a very little book, for all its hundred and twenty poems and pictures; but its covers contain a lyric treasure such as few books, small or great, can boast of.

What renders these little songs so precious is their pure singing quality, what Matthew Arnold calls the "lyrical cry;" and the same quality appears in a really large number of exquisite lyrics scattered throughout Miss Rossetti's volumes; some of them being, perhaps, in the most ethereal and quintessential elements of song, the most perfect we have had since Shelley, whom she resembles also in her free but flawless treatment of rhythm. The peculiar charm of these songs is as distinct and at the same time as immaterial as a perfume. They are fresh with the freshness of dewy grass, or, in their glowing brightness, like a dewdrop turned by the sun into a prism. Thoughtfulness passing into intuition, thoughtfulness that broods as well as sees, and has, like shadowed water, its mysterious depths; this, joined to an extreme yet select simplicity of phrase and a clear and liquid melody of verse, as spontaneous apparently in its outflow as a lark's trill, seems to lie at the root of her lyric art: a careful avoidance of emphasis, a subdued colour and calculated vagueness, aiding often in giving its particular quality to her songs; songs, as a rule, enshrining an almost scentless flower of sentiment.

Finished workmanship, as I intimated at the outset, we find in almost every poem, and workmanship of such calm and even excellence that it is not at first sight we are made aware of the extremely original, thoughtful, and intense nature which throbs so harmoniously beneath it. Even in a poem so full of sorrow and wrath and indignation as the splendid lyric on the German-French campaign, "To-day for Me," a poem that seems written with a pen dipped in the tears of France, no surge of personal feeling disturbs the calm assurance of the rhythm, the solemn reiterance of the tolling burden of rhyme. Indeed, the more deeply or delicately felt the emotion, the more impressive or exquisite, very often, is the art. At the same time, poems like "To-day for Me" are the exception, by no means the rule, in Miss Rossetti's poetry. Something altogether less emphatic must be sought for if we are anxious to find the type, the true representative, of this mystic and remote, yet homely and simple, genius; seeing so deeply into things of the spirit and of nature, overshadowed always with something of a dark imminence of gloom, yet with so large a capacity for joy and simple pleasure; an autumnal muse perhaps, but the muse, certainly, of an autumn going down towards winter with the happy light still on it of a past, or but now scarcely passing, summer.

WILLIAM MORRIS

William Morris, supremely in our time, sought in art only its supreme quality, beauty. He was the pure type of the artist, and, not content with working upon his own craft, the craft of verse, he carried the principles of the artist into many secondary crafts, tapestry, wall-paper, printing, which he made his own, as the artists of the Renaissance made all arts and crafts their own; and, as those artists did, but in another way, he brought life within the scope of art, and willed that life, too, should be beautiful. His very Socialism, as I take it, was but an attempt at weaving the art of life into a beautiful pattern, and giving that beautiful pattern into the hands of poor people, in the hope that they might see its beauty. "Beauty," he once wrote, "which is what is meant by art, using the word in its widest sense, is, I contend, no mere accident of human life, which people can take or leave as they choose, but a positive necessity of life, if we are to live as nature meant us to; that is, unless we are content to be less than men." People did not always realize it; Socialists, I suppose, would realize it a little unwillingly; but to lecture at Hammersmith was more than ever to be the idle singer of an empty day.

"Dreamer of dreams, born out of my due time," he described himself in the prologue to *The Earthly Paradise;* and, indeed, Morris, alone among the poets of our age, was content to be that only, content to spend his days

> making beautiful old rhyme
> In praise of ladies dead and lovely knights.

More than passion, or knowledge, or curiosity, or anything human or divine, he followed beauty, and he was justified of his choice; for his verse has more of the simplicity of beauty than the verse of any English poet since Keats. Where Browning is sometimes cumbered with the care of many important and unessential things; where Tennyson is often lacking through a too fastidious working upon too thin a surface; where Swinburne is carried away by his own music, and Matthew Arnold forgets that he is singing at all; where even Rossetti sometimes accepts strangeness for beauty; there is no temptation strong enough to lure Morris aside from the one path. He had not a great intellect, nor a passionate nature crying to give voice to itself. His most fatal lack was a certain lack of intensity. There is not a great line, there are but few separably fine lines, in the whole of his work. But every line has distinction, and every line is in its place.

Morris was an incomparable story-teller; or, to be precise, he can be compared in our literature only with Chaucer; and it would be rash to say, without premeditation, that Chaucer was a better story-teller than Morris. Chaucer had an incomparably wider range of mastery; he had to his hand the "humours" of all the world. Morris has none of Chaucer's sturdy humanity, his dramatic power, his directness; above all, his humour. But then the aim of Morris was something quite different from the aim of Chaucer, whom I should call the novelist of poets, as Morris was the romance-writer. In several places he has called Chaucer "Master," as in *Life and Death of Jason*:

> O Master, pardon me, if yet in vain
> Thou art my master, and I fail to bring
> Before men's minds the image of the thing
> My heart is filled with.

But in temperament I would compare him rather with Spenser, of whom he has much of the dreamy and picture-weaving vision. Does not this sentence of Landor, describing Spenser, apply singularly well to Morris? "Spenser's is a spacious, but somewhat low chamber, heavy with rich tapestry, on which the figures are mostly disproportioned, but some of the faces are lively and beautiful; the furniture is part creaking and worm-eaten, part fragrant with cedar and sandal-wood and aromatic gums and balsams; every table and mantelpiece and cabinet is covered with gorgeous vases, and birds, and dragons, and houses in the air." This, however, we must except: that in Morris the figures are always in proportion, obey always the lines of conventional design.

To Morris the art of verse was as the art of tapestry; an art of clear design, in which the lines must be simple, and all the beauty must be found in the lines themselves. The words paint pictures; even emotion comes to him as a picture: he sees the lifted arm, tear-stained cheeks, the mouth curving to a smile. Of the words it may be said always that they are happily chosen, not that they are strenuously achieved; they have the grace of being quite the best that could happen, not that fineness which is of long search, rarity, and dear buying. Certainly this was deliberate on his part; and deliberate was his use of the simplest words, which sometimes become a little cloying, and of the simplest rhythms, in which he uses few licences, and almost never attempts an individual effect in any single line; the occasional use of such words as "waking," rhyming to "sing," only adding to the "soft, withdrawing" sound of his fluid cadences. His rhymes are faint, gliding into one another stealthily; dying away, often, upon such vaguely accentuated words as "patiently," "listlessly." He aims at the effect of improvisation, and his verse becomes a sort of pathetic sing-song, like a croon, hardly ever rising or sinking in tone. With its languid, lulling monotony, its "listless chime," it has (especially in those heroic couplets which were finer in his hands than any other measure) the sound of a low plashing of sea-ripples on a quiet shore, a vague and monotonous and continuous and restful going on.

But while he chooses words partly for their gentleness and suave sound, he chooses them far more for their almost unconscious effect of colour; as separate, unimportant stitches in a tapestry, or slabs in a tesselated pavement, to be set together into pictures. His colours, like his designs, are all conventional; he has no half-tones, no subtleties of light and shade; his pictures, indeed, have some of the naïveté which existed before perspective. And as for the hearts and souls of the elegant persons of his pictures, we know them scarcely more than we know the joys and sorrows of an illuminated saint in a missal. These joys and sorrows are all in gold outline, here tender and there sorrowful; but they move us as pictures do, with the delicate and painless emotion of beautiful things. It is all part of the perfumed and cloudy atmosphere of the place, where these dreams wander through their half-existence; this Palace of Art in which life is a coloured and fragrant thing, moving in fine raiment, to the sound of stringed instruments plucked softly.

It is curious, in an art so addressed to the senses, that Morris is so unsensuous in his writing, so modest and temperate, and with so little of the rapture of passionate things. When he achieves a rapture, it is a rapture of sheer beauty; as when the knight Walter first looks upon Venus, "O close, O close there, in the hill's grey shade!" It is when lovers see with each other's eyes, when

the first happy trouble comes into their voices, at
the moment when love first grows aware of itself,
and not yet of the sorrow that is the growth of
love. Tapestry does not appeal to the senses; and
Morris's ideal of beauty, during the main part of
his poetic career, was one in which there was no
room for "violent delights," or any strangeness
that was not tempered to a certain peace, a certain
order. It is his merit that his pictures are always,
as almost no one else's are, exquisitely in keeping
throughout; yet we may reasonably regret that the
intensity which marks many of the pieces in his
first book, *The Defence of Guinevere*, died out in
that first book, and is not to be found again in
his work until *The Story of Sigurd*. He himself
has no interest in the fortunes of his heroes and
heroines when once they step outside the frame of
his picture; in *The Life and Death of Jason* he
leaves Medea, her deadly work done, telling us
merely:

> She came to Athens, and there long did dwell,
> Whose after-life I list not here to tell.

All the world's a picture; and when Paris dies,
crying on Helen,

> yet the sky
> Changed not above his cast-back golden head,
> And merry was the world though he was dead.

To read *Love is Enough*, or *The Earthly Paradise*, or *The Life and Death of Jason*, is like taking opium. One abandons oneself to it, and is borne on clouds as in a gondola of the air. Never was one so gently carried along, so imperceptibly, and with so luxurious a motion. There is not even enough sharpness of interest, or novelty in the progression, to jar one on the way. The only danger is that weariness which comes of overmuch repose.

And Morris at last realized that danger; or, rather, may be said to have satiated himself with his own enchantments. The early influences upon his work had been for the most part mediæval, Chaucer, the Anglo-Norman romances, the new mediævalism of Keats; and always the Odyssey, of which he came to do so fine a translation, so much finer than his translation of the Æneid; the simple picture-words of Homer being so much nearer to him than the jewelled and many-faceted words of Virgil. His first book, which invented a new movement, doing easily, with a certain appropriate quaintness, what Tennyson all his life had been trying to do, has all the exquisite trouble of his first awakening to the love of romance; and he did not again recover quite that naïve thrill of delighted wonder. But the art of almost the whole of his work is a joyous, courtly art; its colour and its sentiment, even when it deals with classical stories, being purely mediæval. The new influence begins to be felt in *The Lovers of Gudrun*, the last tale in the third volume of *The Earthly Paradise*. It is the influence of the Northern Sagas, which took possession of Morris as they took possession of Wagner, both having passed through a period of complete absorption in the knightly and romantic Middle Ages, and both, at the last, going back to the primitive antiquity of legend, and of Northern legend. With Morris, we feel that certain energies, latent in the man from the first, and, indeed, compressed within certain limits by the exercise of a most energetic will, have at last been allowed free play. The simple, artificial English of the earlier books gives place to a new, and in a sense not less artificial, style, returning upon earlier English models, and forging for itself monosyllabic words which are themselves energies. In *The Story of Sigurd*, which remains his masterpiece of sustained power, he goes sheer through civilization, and finds an ampler beauty shadowed under the dusk of the Gods. He gets a larger style, a style more rooted in the earth, more vivid with the impulse of nature; and the beauty of his writing is now a grave beauty, from which all mere prettiness is clean consumed away. And now, at last, he touches the heart; for he sings of the passions of men, of the fierceness of love and hate, of the music of swords in the day of battle. And still, more than ever, he is the poet of beauty; for he has realized that in beauty there is something more elemental than smiling lips, or the soft dropping of tears.

COVENTRY PATMORE

THE most austere poet of our time, Coventry Patmore conceived of art as a sort of abstract ecstasy, whose source, limit, and end are that supreme wisdom which is the innermost essence of love. Thus the whole of his work, those "bitter, sweet, few, and veil'd" songs, which are the fruit of two out of his seventy years, is love-poetry; and it is love-poetry of a quite unique kind. In the earlier of his two books, *The Angel in the House*, we see him, in the midst of a scientific generation (in which it was supposed that by adding prose to poetry you doubled the value of poetry) unable to escape the influence of his time, desperately set on doing the wrong thing by design, yet unable to keep himself from often doing the right thing by accident. In his later book, *The Unknown Eros*, he has achieved the proper recognition of himself, the full consciousness of the means to his own end; and it is by *The Unknown Eros* that he will live, if it is enough claim to immortality to have written the most devout, subtle, and sublimated love-poetry of our century.

Patmore tells us in *The Angel in the House*, that it was his intention to write

> That hymn for which the whole world longs,
> A worthy hymn in woman's praise.

But at that time his only conception of woman was the conception of woman as the lady. Now poetry has nothing whatever to do with woman as the lady; it is in the novel, the comedy of manners, that we expect the society of ladies. Prose, in the novel and the drama, is at liberty to concern itself with those secondary emotions which come into play in our familiar intercourse with one another; with those conventions which are the "evening dress" by which our varying temperaments seek the disguise of an outward uniformity; with those details of life which are also, in a sense, details of costume, and thus of value to the teller of a tale, the actor on a stage. But the poet who endeavours to bring all this machinery of prose into the narrow and self-sufficing limits of verse is as fatally doomed to failure as the painter who works after photographs, instead of from the living model. At the time when *The Angel* was written, the heresy of the novel in verse was in the air. Were there not, before and after it, the magnificent failure of *Aurora Leigh*, the ineffectual, always interesting, endeavours of Clough, and certain more careful, more sensitive, never quite satisfactory, experiments of Tennyson? Patmore went his own way, to a more ingenious failure than any. *The Angel in the House* is written with exquisite neatness, occasional splendour; it is the very flower of the poetry of convention; and is always lifting the trivialities and the ingenuities to which, for the most part, it restricts itself, miraculously near to that height which, now and again, in such lines as "The Revelation," it fully attains. But it is not here, it is in *The Unknown Eros* alone, that Patmore has given immortality to what is immortal in perishable things.

How could it be otherwise, when the whole force of the experiment lies in the endeavour to say essentially unpoetical things in a poetical manner?

> Give me the power of saying things
> Too simple and too sweet for words,

was his wise, reasonable, and afterwards answered prayer. Was it after the offering of such a prayer that he wrote of

> Briggs,
> Factotum, Footman, Butler, Groom?

But it is not merely of such "vulgar errors" as this that we have to complain, it is of the very success, the indisputable achievement, of all but the most admirable parts of the poem. The subtlety, the fineness of analysis, the simplified complexity, of such things as "The Changed Allegiance," can scarcely be overpraised as studies in "the dreadful heart of woman," from the point of view of a shrewd, kindly, somewhat condescending, absolutely clear-eyed observer, so dispassionate that he has not even the privilege of an illusion, so impartial that you do not even do his fervour the compliment of believing it possible that his perfect Honoria had, after all, defects. But in all this, admirable as it is, there is nothing which could not have been as well said in prose. It is the point of view of the egoist, of the " marrying man," to whom

> Each beauty blossomed in the sight
> Of tender personal regards.

Woman is observed always in reference to the man who fancies she may prove worthy to be his " predestinated mate," and it seems to him his highest boast that he is

>   proud
> To take his passion into church.

At its best, this is the poetry of "being in love," not of love; of affection, not passion. Passion is a thing of flame, rarely burning pure, or without danger to him that holds that wind-blown torch in his hand; while affection, such as this legalized affection of *The Angel in the House*, is a gentle and comfortable warmth, as of a hearth-side. It is that excellent, not quite essential, kind of love which need endure neither pain nor revolt; for it has conquered the world on the world's terms.

Woman, as she is seen in *The Angel in the House*, is a delightful, adorable, estimable, prettily capricious child; demonstrably finite, capturable, a butterfly not yet Psyche. It is the severest judgment on her poet that she is never a mystery to him. For all art is founded on mystery, and to the poet, as to the child, the whole world is mysterious. There are experts who tell me that this world, and life, and the flowing of times past into times to come, are but a simple matter after all: the jarring of this atom against that, a growth by explicable degrees from a germ perhaps not altogether inexplicable. And there are the experts in woman, who will explain to me the bright disarray of her caprices, the strangeness of her moods, the unreason of her sway over man; assuring me that she is mysterious only because she is not seen through, and that she can never be seen through because into the depths of emptiness one can see but a little distance. Not of such is the true lover, the true poet. To him woman is as mysterious as the night of stars, and all he learns of her is but to deepen the mystery which surrounds her as with clouds. To him she is Fate, an unconscious part of what is eternal in things; and, being the liveliest image of beauty, she is to be reverenced for her beauty, as the saints are reverenced for their virtue. What is it to me if you tell me that she is but the creature of a day, prized for her briefness, as we prize flowers; loved for her egoism, as we love infants; marvelled at for the exquisite and audacious completeness of her ignorance? Or what is it to me if you tell me that she is all that a lady should be, infinitely perfect in pettiness; and that her choice will reward the calculations of a gentleman? If she is not a flame, devouring and illuminating, and if your passion for her is not as another consuming and refining flame, each rushing into either that both may be commingled in a brighter ecstasy, you have not seen woman as it is the joy of the poet and the lover to see her; and your fine distinctions, your disentangling of sensations, your subtleties of interpretation, will be at the best but of the subject of prose, revealing to me what is transitory in the eternal rather than what is eternal in the transitory. The art of Coventry Patmore, in *The Angel in the House*, is an art founded on this scientific conception of woman. But the poet, who began by thinking of woman as being at her best a perfect lady, ended by seeing her seated a little higher than the angels, at the right hand of the Madonna, of whom indeed she is a scarcely lower symbol. She who was a bright and cherished toy in *The Angel in the House* becomes in *The Unknown Eros* pure spirit, the passionate sister of the pure idea. She is the mystical rose of beauty, the female half of that harmony of opposites which is God. She has other names, and is the Soul, the Church, the Madonna. To be her servant is to be the servant of all right, the enemy of all wrong; and therefore poems of fierce patriotism, and disdainful condemnation of the foolish and vulgar who are the adversaries of God's ordinances and man's, find their appropriate place among poems of tender human pathos, of ecstatic human and divine love. And she is now, at last, apprehended under her most essential aspect, as the supreme mystery; and her worship becomes an almost secret ritual, of which none but the adepts can fathom the full significance.

Vision, in *The Unknown Eros*, is too swift, immediate, and far-seeing to be clouded by the delicate veils of dreams.

> Give me the steady heat
> Of thought wise, splendid, sweet,
> Urged by the great, rejoicing wind that rings
> With draught of unseen wings,
> Making each phrase, for love and for delight,
> Twinkle like Sirius on a frosty night:

that is his prayer, and it was not needful for him to

> remain
> Content to ask unlikely gifts in vain.

Out of this love-poetry all but the very essence of passion has been consumed; and love is seen to be the supreme wisdom, even more than the supreme delight. Apprehended on every side, and with the same controlling ardour, those "frightful nuptials" of the Dove and Snake, which are one of his allegories, lead upward, on the wings of an almost aërial symbolism, to those all but inaccessible heights where mortal love dies into that intense, self-abnegating, intellectual passion, which we name the love of God.

At this height, at its very highest, his art becomes abstract ecstasy. It was one of his contentions, in that beautiful book of prose, *Religio Poetæ*, in which thought is sustained throughout at almost the lyrical pitch, that the highest art is not emotional, and that "the music of Handel, the poetry of Æschylus, and the architecture of the Parthenon are appeals to a sublime good sense which takes scarcely any account of 'the emotions.'" Not the highest art only, but all art, if it is so much as to come into existence, must be emotional; for it is only emotion which puts life into the deathlike slumber of words, of stones, of the figures on a clef. But emotion may take any shape, may inform the least likely of substances. Is not all music a kind of divine mathematics, and is not mathematics itself a rapture to the true adept? To Patmore abstract things were an emotion, became indeed the highest emotion of which he was capable; and that joy, which he notes as the mark of fine art, that peace, which to him was the sign of great art, themselves the most final of the emotions, interpenetrated for him the whole substance of thought, aspiration, even argument. Never were arguments at once so metaphysical and so mystical, so precise, analytic, and passionate as those "high arguments" which fill these pages with so thrilling a life.

The particular subtlety of Patmore's mysticism finds perhaps its counterpart in the writings of certain of the Catholic mystics: it has at once the clear-eyed dialectic of the Schoolmen and the august heat of St. Teresa. Here is passion which analyzes itself, and yet with so passionate a complexity that it remains passion. Read, for instance, that eulogy of "Pain," which is at once a lyric rapture, and betrays an almost unholy depth of acquaintance with the hidden, tortuous, and delightful ways of sensation. Read that song of songs, "Deliciæ Sapientiæ de Amore," which seems to speak, with the tongue of angels, all the secrets of all those "to whom generous Love, by any name, is dear." Read that other, interrupted song,

> Building new bulwarks 'gainst the infinite,

"Legem tuam dilexi." Read those perhaps less quintessential dialogues in which a personified Psyche seeks wisdom of Eros and the Pythoness. And then, if you would realize how subtle an argument in verse may be, how elegantly and happily expressed, and yet not approach, at its highest climb, the point from which these other arguments in verse take flight, turn to *The Angel in the House*, and read "The Changed Allegiance." The difference is the difference between wisdom and worldly wisdom: wisdom being the purified and most ardent emotion of the intellect, and thus of the very essence of poetry; while worldly wisdom is but the dispassionate ingenuity of the intelligence, and thus of not so much as the highest substance of prose.

The word "glittering," which Patmore so frequently uses, and always with words which soften its sharpness, may be applied, not unsuitably, to much of his writing in this book: a "glittering peace" does indeed seem to illuminate it. The writing throughout is classical, in a sense in which perhaps no other writing of our time is classical. When he says of the Virgin:

> Therefore, holding a little thy soft breath,
> Thou underwent'st the ceremony of death;

or, of the eternal paradox of love :

> 'Tis but in such captivity
> The unbounded Heavens know what they be;

when he cries :
> O Love, that, like a rose,
> Deckest my breast with beautiful repose;

or speaks of "this fond indignity, delight"; he is, though with an entirely personal accent, writing in the purest classical tradition. He was accustomed always, in his counsels to young writers, to reiterate that saying of Aristotle, that in the language of poetry there should be "a continual slight novelty"; and I remember that he would point to his own work, with that legitimate pride in himself which was one of the fierce satisfactions of his somewhat lonely and unacknowledged old age. There is in every line of *The Unknown Eros* that continual slight novelty which makes classical poetry, certainly, classical. Learned in every metre, Patmore never wrote but in one, the iambic: and there was a similar restraint, a similar refusal of what was good, but not (as he conceived) the highest good, all strangeness of beauty, all trouble, curiosity, the splendour of excess, in the words and substance of his writing. I find no exception even in that fiercely aristocratic political verse, which is the very rapture of indignation and wrath against such things as seemed to him worthy to be hated of God.

Like Landor, with whom he had other points of resemblance, Coventry Patmore was a good hater. May one not say, like all great lovers? He hated the mob, because he saw in it the "amorous and vehement drift of man's herd to hell." He hated Protestantism, because he saw in it a weakening of the bonds of spiritual order. He hated the Protestantism of modern art, its revolt against the tradition of the "true Church," the many heresies of its many wanderings after a strange, perhaps forbidden, beauty. Art was to him religion, as religion was to him the supreme art. He was a mystic who found in Catholicism the sufficing symbols of those beliefs which were the deepest emotions of his spirit. It was a necessity to him to be dogmatic, and he gave to even his petulances the irresistible sanction of the Church.

WALTER PATER

WALTER PATER was a man in whom fineness and subtlety of emotion were united with an exact and profound scholarship; in whom a personality singularly unconventional, and singularly full of charm, found for its expression an absolutely personal and an absolutely novel style, which was the most carefully and curiously beautiful of all English styles. The man and his style, to those who knew him, were identical; for, as his style was unlike that of other men, concentrated upon a kind of perfection which, for the most part, they could not even distinguish, so his inner life was peculiarly his own, centred within a circle beyond which he refused to wander; his mind, to quote some words of his own, "keeping as a solitary prisoner its own dream of a world." And he was the most lovable of men; to those who rightly apprehended him, the most fascinating; the most generous and helpful of private friends, and in literature a living counsel of perfection, whose removal seems to leave modern English prose without a contemporary standard of values.

"For it is with the delicacies of fine literature

especially, its gradations of expression, its fine judgment, its pure sense of words, of vocabulary —things, alas! dying out in the English literature of the present, together with the appreciation of them in our literature of the past—that his literary mission is chiefly concerned." These words, applied by Pater to Charles Lamb, might reasonably enough have been applied to himself; especially in that earlier part of his work, which remains to me, as I doubt not it remains to many others, the most entirely delightful. As a critic, he selected for analysis only those types of artistic character in which delicacy, an exquisite fineness, is the principal attraction; or if, as with Michel Angelo, he was drawn towards some more rugged personality, some more massive, less finished art, it was not so much from sympathy with these more obvious qualities of ruggedness and strength, but because he had divined the sweetness lying at the heart of the strength: "ex forti dulcedo." Leonardo da Vinci, Joachim du Bellay, Coleridge, Botticelli: we find always something a little exotic, or subtle, or sought out, a certain rarity, which it requires an effort to disengage, and which appeals for its perfect appreciation to a public within the public; those fine students of what is fine in art, who take their artistic pleasures consciously, deliberately, critically, with the learned love of the amateur.

And not as a critic only, judging others, but in his own person as a writer, both of critical and of imaginative work, Pater showed his preoccupation with the "delicacies of fine literature." His prose was from the first conscious, and it was from the first perfect. That earliest book of his, *Studies in the History of the Renaissance*, as it was then called, entirely individual, the revelation of a rare and special temperament, though it was, had many affinities with the poetic and pictorial art of Rossetti, Mr. Swinburne, and Burne Jones, and seems, on its appearance in 1873, to have been taken as the manifesto of the so-called "æsthetic" school. And, indeed, it may well be compared, as artistic prose, with the poetry of Rossetti; as fine, as careful, as new a thing as that, and with something of the same exotic odour about it: a savour in this case of French soil, a Watteau grace and delicacy. Here was criticism as a fine art, written in prose which the reader lingered over as over poetry; modulated prose which made the splendour of Mr. Ruskin seem gaudy, the neatness of Matthew Arnold a mincing neatness, and the brass sound strident in the orchestra of Carlyle.

That book of *Studies in the Renaissance*, even with the rest of Pater to choose from, seems to me sometimes to be the most beautiful book of prose in our literature. Nothing in it is left to inspiration: but it is all inspired. Here is a writer who, like Baudelaire, would better nature; and in this goldsmith's work of his prose he too has "rêvé le miracle d'une prose poétique, musicale sans rhythme et sans rime." An almost oppressive quiet, a quiet which seems to exhale an atmosphere heavy with the odour of tropical flowers, broods over these pages; a subdued light shadows them. The most felicitous touches come we know not whence, "a breath, a flame in the doorway, a feather in the wind;" here are the simplest words, but they take colour from each other by the cunning accident of their placing in the sentence, "the subtle spiritual fire kindling from word to word."

In this book prose seemed to have conquered a new province; and further, along this direction, prose could not go. Twelve years later, when *Marius the Epicurean* appeared, it was in a less coloured manner of writing that the "sensations and ideas" of that reticent, wise, and human soul were given to the world. Here and there, perhaps, the goldsmith, adding more value, as he thought, for every trace of gold that he removed, might seem to have scraped a little too assiduously. But the style of *Marius*, in its more arduous self-repression, has a graver note, and brings with it a severer kind of beauty. Writers who have paid particular attention to style have often been accused of caring little *what* they say, knowing how beautifully they can say anything. The accusation has generally been unjust: as if any fine beauty could be but skin-deep! The merit which, more than any other, distinguishes Pater's prose, though it is not the merit most on the surface, is the attention to, the perfection of, the ensemble. Under the soft and musical phrases an inexorable logic hides itself, sometimes only too well. Link is added silently, but faultlessly, to link; the argument marches, carrying you with it, while you fancy you are only listening to the music with which it keeps step. Take an essay to pieces, and you will find that it is constructed with mathematical precision; every piece can be taken out and replaced in order. I do not know any contemporary writer who observes the logical requirements so scrupulously, who conducts an argument so steadily from deliberate point to point towards a determined goal. And here, in *Marius*, which is not a story, but the philosophy of a soul, this art of the ensemble is not less rigorously satisfied; though indeed *Marius* is but a sequence of scenes, woven around a sequence of moods.

In this book, and in the *Imaginary Portraits* of three years later, which seems to me to show his imaginative and artistic faculties at their point of most perfect fusion, Pater has not endeavoured to create characters, in whom the flesh and blood should seem to be that of life itself; he had not the energy of creation, and he was content with a more shadowy life than theirs for the children of his dreams. What he has done is to give a concrete form to abstract ideas; to represent certain types of character, to trace certain developments, in the picturesque form of narrative; to which, indeed, the term portrait is very happily applied; for the method is that of a very patient and elaborate brush-work, in which the touches that go to form the likeness are so fine that it is difficult to see quite their individual value, until, the end being reached, the whole picture starts out before you. Each, with perhaps one exception, is the study of a soul, or rather of a consciousness; such a study as might be made by simply looking within, and projecting now this now that side of oneself on an exterior plane. I do not mean to say that I attribute to Pater himself the philosophical theories of Sebastian van Storck, or the artistic ideals of Duke Carl of Rosenmold. I mean that the attitude of mind, the outlook, in the most general sense, is always limited and directed in a certain way, giving one always the picture of a delicate, subtle, aspiring, unsatisfied personality, open to all impressions, living chiefly by sensations, little anxious to reap any of the rich harvest of its intangible but keenly possessed gains; a personality withdrawn from action, which it despises or dreads, solitary with its ideals, in the circle of its "exquisite moments," in the Palace of Art, where it is never quite at rest. It is somewhat such a soul, I have thought, as that which Browning has traced in *Sordello;* indeed, when reading for the first time *Marius the Epicurean* I was struck by a certain resemblance between the record of the sensations and ideas of Marius of White-Nights and that of the sensations and events of Sordello of Goito.

The style of the *Imaginary Portraits* is the

ripest, the most varied and flawless, their art the most assured and masterly, of any of Pater's books: it was the book that he himself preferred in his work, thinking it, to use his own phrase, more "natural" than any other. And of the four portraits the most wonderful seems to me the poem, for it is really a poem, named "Denys l'Auxerrois." For once, it is not the study of a soul, but of a myth; a transposition (in which one hardly knows whether to admire most the learning, the ingenuity, or the subtle imagination) of that strangest myth of the Greeks, the "Pagan after-thought" of Dionysus Zagreus, into the conditions of mediæval life. Here is prose so coloured, so modulated, as to have captured, along with almost every sort of poetic richness, and in a rhythm which is essentially the rhythm of prose, even the suggestiveness of poetry, that most volatile and unseizable property, of which prose has so rarely been able to possess itself. The style of "Denys l'Auxerrois" has a subdued heat, a veiled richness of colour, which contrasts curiously with the silver-grey coolness of "A Prince of Court Painters," the chill, more leaden grey of "Sebastian van Storck," though it has a certain affinity, perhaps, with the more variously-tinted canvas of "Duke Carl of Rosenmold." Watteau, Sebastian, Carl: unsatisfied seekers, all of them, this after an artistic ideal of impossible perfection, that after a chill and barren ideal of philosophic thinking and living, that other after yet another ideal, unattainable to him in his period, of life "im Ganzen, Guten, Schönen," a beautiful and effective culture. The story of each, like that of *Marius* is a vague tragedy, ending abruptly, after so many uncertainties, and always with some subtly ironic effect in the accident of its conclusion. The mirror is held up to Watteau while he struggles desperately or hesitatingly forward, snatching from art one after another of her reticent secrets; then, with a stroke, it is broken, and this artist in immortal things sinks out of sight, into a narrow grave of red earth. The mirror is held up to Sebastian as he moves deliberately, coldly, onward in the midst of a warm life which has so little attraction for him, freeing himself one by one from all obstructions to a clear philosophic equilibrium; and the mirror is broken, with a like suddenness, and the seeker disappears from our sight; to find, perhaps, what he had sought. It is held up to Duke Carl, the seeker after the satisfying things of art and experience, the dilettante in material and spiritual enjoyment, the experimenter on life; and again it is broken, with an almost terrifying shock, just as he is come to a certain rash crisis: is it a step upward or downward? a step, certainly, towards the concrete, towards a possible material felicity.

We see Pater as an imaginative writer, pure and simple, only in these two books, *Marius* and the *Imaginary Portraits*, in the unfinished romance of *Gaston de Latour* (in which detail had already begun to obscure the outlines of the central figure) and in those *Imaginary Portraits* reprinted in various volumes, but originally intended to form a second series under that title: "Hippolytus Veiled," "Apollo in Picardy," "Emerald Uthwart"; and that early first chapter of an unwritten story of modern English life, "The Child in the House." For the rest, he was content to be a critic: a critic of poetry and painting in the *Studies in the Renaissance* and the *Appreciations*, of sculpture and the arts of life in the *Greek Studies*, of philosophy in the volume on *Plato and Platonism*. But he was a critic as no one else ever was a critic. He had made a fine art of criticism. His criticism, abounding in the close and strenuous qualities of really earnest judgment, grappling with his subject as if there were nothing to do but that, the "fine writing" in it being largely mere conscientiousness in providing a subtle and delicate thought with words as subtle and delicate, was, in effect, written with as scrupulous a care, with as much artistic finish, as much artistic purpose, as any imaginative work whatever; being indeed, in a sense in which, perhaps, no other critical work is, imaginative work itself.

" The æsthetic critic," we are told in the preface to the *Studies in the Renaissance*, "regards all the objects with which he has to do, all works of art, and the fairer forms of nature and human life, as powers or forces producing pleasurable sensations, each of a more or less peculiar and unique kind. This influence he feels, and wishes to explain, analyzing it, and reducing it to its elements. To him, the picture, the landscape, the engaging personality in life or in a book, *La Gioconda*, the hills of Carrara, Pico of Mirandola, are valuable for their virtues, as we say in speaking of a herb, a wine, a gem; for the property each has of affecting one with a special, a unique, impression of pleasure." To this statement of what was always the aim of Pater in criticism, I would add, from the later essay on Wordsworth, a further statement, applying it, as he there does, to the criticism of literature. "What special sense," he asks, "does Wordsworth exercise, and what instincts does he satisfy? What are the subjects which in him excite the imaginative faculty? What are the qualities in things and persons which he values, the impression and sense of which he can convey to others, in an extraordinary way?" How far is this ideal from that old theory, not yet extinct, which has been briefly stated, thus, by Edgar Poe: "While the critic is *permitted* to play, at times, the part of the mere commentator—while he is *allowed*, by way of merely *interesting* his readers, to put in the fairest light the merits of his author—his *legitimate* task is still, in pointing out and analyzing defects, and showing how the work might have been improved, to aid the cause of letters, without undue heed of the individual literary men." And Poe goes on to protest, energetically, against the more merciful (and how infinitely more fruitful!) principles of Goethe, who held that what it concerns us to know about a work or a writer are the merits, not the defects, of the writer and the work. Pater certainly carried this theory to its furthest possible limits, and may almost be said never, except by implication, to condemn anything. But then the force of this implication testifies to a fastidiousness infinitely greater than that of the most destructive of the destructive critics. Is it necessary to *say* that one dislikes a thing? It need but be ignored; and Pater ignored whatever did not come up to his very exacting standard, finding quite enough to write about in that small residue which remained over.

Nor did he merely ignore what was imperfect, he took the further step, the taking of which was what made him a creative artist in criticism. "It was thus," we are told of Gaston de Latour, in one of the chapters of the unfinished romance, "it was thus Gaston understood the poetry of Ronsard, *generously expanding it to the full measure of its intention.*" That is precisely what Pater does in his criticisms, in which criticism is a divining-rod over hidden springs. He has a unique faculty of seeing, through every imperfection, the perfect work, the work as the artist saw it, as he strove to make it, as he failed, in his measure, quite adequately to achieve it. He goes straight to what is fundamental, the true root of the matter, leaving all the rest out of the question. The essay on Wordsworth is perhaps the best example of this, for it has fallen to the lot of Wordsworth to suffer more than most at the hands of interpreters. Here, at last, is a critic who can see in him "a poet somewhat bolder and more passionate than might at first sight be supposed, but not too bold for true poetical taste; an unimpassioned writer, you might sometimes fancy, yet thinking the chief aim, in life and art alike, to be a certain deep emotion;" one whose "words are themselves thought and feeling;" "a master, an expert, in the art of impassioned contemplation." Reading such essays as these, it is difficult not to feel that if Lamb and Wordsworth, if Shakespeare, if Sir Thomas Browne, could but come to life again for the pleasure of reading them, that pleasure would be the sensation: "Here is someone who understands just what I meant to do, what was almost too deep in me for expression, and would have, I knew, to be divined; that something, scarcely expressed in any of my words, without which no word I ever wrote would have been written."

Turning from the criticisms of literature to the studies on painting, we see precisely the same qualities, but not, I think, precisely the same results. In a sentence of the essay on "The School of Giorgione," which is perhaps the most nicely-balanced of all his essays on painting, he defines, with great precision: "In its primary aspect, a

great picture has no more definite message for us
than an accidental play of sunlight and shadow for a
moment on the floor: is itself in truth a space of
such fallen light, caught as the colours are caught in
an Eastern carpet, but refined upon, and dealt with
more subtly and exquisitely than by nature itself."
But for the most part it was not in this spirit that he
wrote of pictures. His criticism of pictures is indeed
creative, in a fuller sense than his criticism of books;
and, in the necessity of things, dealing with an art
which, as he admitted, has, in its primary aspect, no
more definite message for us than the sunlight on
the floor, he not merely divined, but also added, out
of the most sympathetic knowledge, certainly. It is
one thing to interpret the meaning of a book; quite
another to interpret the meaning of a picture. Take,
for instance, the essay on Botticelli. That was the
first sympathetic study of at that time a little-known
painter which had appeared in English; and it contains some of Pater's most exquisite writing. All
that he writes, of those Madonnas "who are neither
for Jehovah nor for His enemies," of that sense in
the painter of "the wistfulness of exiles," represents,
certainly, the impression made upon his own mind
by these pictures, and, as such, has an interpretative
value, apart from its beauty as a piece of writing.
But it is after all a speculation before a canvas, a
literary fantasy; a possible interpretation, if you
will, of one mood in the painter, a single side of his
intention; it is not a criticism, inevitable as that

criticism of Wordsworth's art, of the art of Botticelli.

This once understood, we must admit that Pater did more than anyone of our time to bring about a more intimate sympathy with some of the subtler aspects of art; that his influence did much to rescue us from the dangerous moralities, the uncritical enthusiasms and prejudices, of Mr. Ruskin; that of no other art-critic it could be said that his taste was flawless. And in regard to his treatment of sculpture, we may say more; for here we can speak without reservations. In those essays on "The Beginnings of Greek Sculpture," and the rest, he has made sculpture a living, intimate, thing; and, with no addition of his fancy, but in a minute, learned, intuitive piecing together of little fact by little fact, has shown its growth, its relation to life, its meaning in art. I find much of the same quality in his studies in Greek myths: that coloured, yet so scrupulous "Study of Dionysus," the patient disentanglings of the myth of Demeter and Persephone. And, in what is the latest work, practically, that we have from his hand, the lectures on *Plato and Platonism*, we see a like scrupulous and discriminating judgment brought to bear, as upon an artistic problem, upon the problems of Greek ethics, Greek philosophy.

"Philosophy itself indeed, as he conceives it," Pater tells us, speaking of Plato (he might be speaking of himself) "is but the systematic appreciation of a kind of music in the very nature of things." And philosophy, as he conceives it, is a living, dramatic thing, among personalities, and the strife of temperaments; a doctrine being seen as a vivid fragment of some very human mind, not a dry matter of words and disembodied reason. "In the discussion even of abstract truth," he reminds us, "it is not so much what he thinks as the person who is thinking, that after all really tells." Thus, the student's duty, in reading Plato, "is not to take his side in a controversy, to adopt or refute Plato's opinions, to modify, or make apology for what may seem erratic or impossible in him; still less, to furnish himself with arguments on behalf of some theory or conviction of his own. His duty is rather to follow intelligently, but with strict indifference, the mental process there, as he might witness a game of skill; better still, as in reading *Hamlet* or *The Divine Comedy*, so in reading *The Republic*, to watch, for its dramatic interest, the spectacle of a powerful, of a sovereign intellect, translating itself, amid a complex group of conditions which can never in the nature of things occur again, at once pliant and resistant to them, into a great literary monument." It is thus that Pater studies his subject, with an extraordinary patience and precision; a patience with ideas, not, at first sight, so clear or so interesting as he induces them to become; a precision of thinking, on his part, in which no licence is ever permitted to the fantastic side-issues of things. Here again we have criticism which, in its divination, its arrangement, its building up of many materials into a living organism, is itself creation, becomes imaginative work itself.

We may seem to be far now, but are not in reality so far as it may seem, from those "delicacies of fine literature," with which I began by showing Pater to be so greatly concerned. And, in considering the development by which a writer who had begun with the *Studies in the Renaissance* ended with *Plato and Platonism*, we must remember, as Mr. Gosse has so acutely pointed out in his valuable study of Pater's personal characteristics, that, after all, it was philosophy which attracted him before either literature or art, and that his first published essay was an essay on Coleridge, in which Coleridge the metaphysician, and not Coleridge the poet, was the interesting person to him. In his return to an early, and one might think, in a certain sense, immature interest, it need not surprise us to find a development, which I cannot but consider as technically something of a return to a primitive lengthiness and involution, towards a style which came to lose many of the rarer qualities of its perfect achievement. I remember that when he once said to me that the *Imaginary Portraits* seemed to him the best written of his books, he qualified that very just appreciation by adding: "It seems to me the most *natural*." I think he was even then beginning to forget that it was not natural to him to be natural. There are in the world many kinds of beauty, and of these what is called natural beauty is but one. Pater's temperament was at once shy and complex, languid and ascetic, sensuous and spiritual. He did not permit life to come to him without a certain ceremony; he was on his guard against the abrupt indiscretion of events; and if his whole life was a service of art, he arranged his life so that, as far as possible, it might be served by that very dedication. With this conscious ordering of things, it became a last sophistication to aim at an effect in style which should bring the touch of unpremeditation, which we seem to find in nature, into a faultlessly combined arrangement of art. The lectures on Plato, really spoken, show traces of their actual delivery in certain new, vocal effects, which had begun already to interest him as matters of style; and which we may find, more finely, here and there in *Gaston de Latour*. Perhaps all this was but a pausing-place in a progress. That it would not have been the final stage, we may be sure. But it is idle to speculate what further development awaited, at its own leisure, so incalculable a life.

MODERNITY IN VERSE

In the poetry of Mr. Henley, so interesting always, and at times so admirable, I find an example to my hand of the quality of modernity in verse. For a man of such active and eager temperament, a writer of such intellectual vivacity, Mr. Henley's literary baggage is singularly small. It consists of two volumes of verse, a volume of prose criticisms, some essays about painting, a few prefaces, and one or two plays written in collaboration with Robert Louis Stevenson. To these we should perhaps add the *National Observer*, a weekly paper written in collaboration with a number of impressionable young men. Ten years ago Mr. Henley's name was unknown. Journalists knew him as a clever journalist, and that was all. It was only by an accident that the editor (at that time) of the *Magazine of Art*, the brilliant reviewer of the *Athenæum*, was discovered by the general public in the character of a poet. The accident was somewhat curious. In 1887 a volume of *Ballades and Rondeaus* appeared in the Canterbury Series under the editorship of Mr. Gleeson White. It was a collection of all the tolerable

MODERNITY IN VERSE

work in French forms that could be found in English and American literature, and its consequence (for our salvation) was such an indigestion of ingenuity that scarcely a ballade, scarcely a rondeau, has seen the light since its publication. As a curiosity the book had its interest; containing, as it did, some of the splendid work of Mr. Swinburne, the exquisite work of Mr. Dobson, it could not but have its value; but, after all, its main interest and value lay in some five-and-thirty pieces signed W. E. Henley. Mr. Gleeson White explained in his preface that he had discovered these pieces in a society paper called *London*, a paper which had two years of a very vivid existence during 1877-78, and that he had made his selection without the slightest idea that they were all by one author, and that author Mr. Henley. Written in the artificial forms of the ballade, the rondeau, the villanelle, they stood out from a mass of work, mainly artificial in substance as in form, by the freshness of their inspiration, the joyous individuality of their note. One felt that here was a new voice, and a voice with capacities for a better kind of singing. It was in answer to a demand which would take no denying (and how rarely does the British public ever make such a demand!) that *A Book of Verses* appeared in the following year. It was a complete success, was welcomed by the critics, talked about in the drawing-rooms, and even bought for ready money. In 1890 a volume of *Views and Reviews* was received with much curiosity, as a challenge that at all events had to be considered. In 1891 the play of *Beau Austin* (the work of Mr. Henley and Mr. Stevenson) was the literary sensation of the dramatic year, and, though not exactly a success on the boards, must be admitted to have presented to us the finest piece of comedy in action since *The School for Scandal*. And then, in 1892, came *The Song of the Sword*, or, as it is now more appropriately named, *London Voluntaries*, another challenge, and, in some sort, a manifesto.

There is something revolutionary about all Mr. Henley's work; the very titles, the very existence, of his poems may be taken as a sort of manifesto on behalf of what is surely a somewhat new art, the art of modernity in verse. In the *London Voluntaries*, for instance, what a sense of the poetry of cities, that rarer than pastoral poetry, the romance of what lies beneath our eyes, in the humanity of streets, if we have but the vision and the point of view! Here, at last, is a poet who can so enlarge the limits of his verse as to take in London. And I think that might be the test of poetry which professes to be modern: its capacity for dealing with London, with what one sees or might see there, indoors and out.

To be modern in poetry, to represent really oneself and one's surroundings, the world as it is to-day, to be modern and yet poetical, is, perhaps, the most difficult, as it is certainly the most interesting, of all artistic achievements. In music the modern soul seems to have found expression in Wagner; in painting it may be said to have taken form and colour in Manet, Degas, and Whistler; in sculpture, has it not revealed itself in Rodin? on the stage it is certainly typified in Sarah Bernhardt. Essentially modern poetry may be said to have begun in France, with Baudelaire. The art which he invented, a perverse, self-scrutinizing, troubled art of sensation and nerves, has been yet further developed, subtilized, volatilized, rather, by Verlaine, who still remains the typical modern poet. In England we find the first suggestions of a really modern conception of poetical art in some of the smaller and finer poems of Browning. Mr. George Meredith's *Modern Love* almost realizes an ideal. The poem stands alone in the literature of its time; moving by "tragic hints," to the cadence of an irony that achieves a quite new expression in verse, it gives voice, in that acid, stinging, bitter-sweet style made out of the very moods of these modern lovers, to all that is new, troubled, unexpressed, in the convolutions of passion, all that is strange, novel, and unexpected, in the accidents of passionate situation, among our sophisticated lovers of to-day. In quite another way Mr. Coventry Patmore has achieved wonders, not in the domestic *Angel,* but in the less popular and immeasurably superior *Unknown Eros,* by working, with that extraordinarily delicate touch of his, on the emotions and destinies of the more spiritual kind of love, which is no less, in essentials and accidentals alike, "modern love." Had Walt Whitman only possessed the art, as he possessed, and at times revealed, the soul of poetry, it is possible that in him we should have found the typical modern poet. But his work remains a suggestion, not an accomplishment. In James Thomson we find a violent and inconsiderate attempt to deal with modern subjects, often in an old-fashioned way. He was a man of genius who never found the right utterance, but his endeavour was in the right direction. He indeed aimed at doing much of what Mr. Henley seems to me to have actually done.

To some of the writers I have named, and to some others, Mr. Henley owes not a little. The style of the "Hospital Sonnets" is founded on the style of *Modern Love*; both from the rhymed and unrhymed poems in irregular metres, it is evident that Mr. Henley has learnt something from the odes of the *Unknown Eros*; there are touches of Walt Whitman, some of the notes of Heine; there is, too, something of the exquisitely disarticulated style of Verlaine. But with all this assimilation of influences that are in the air, Mr. Henley has developed for himself a style that becomes in the highest degree personal, and one realizes behind it a most vigorous, distinct, and interesting personality. Alike as a human document, and as an artistic experiment, the "rhymes and rhythms" named "In Hospital" have a peculiar value. Dated from the Old Edinburgh Infirmary, 1873-75, they tell the story of life in hospital, from the first glimpse of the "tragic meanness" of stairs and corridors, through the horrors of the operation, by way of visitors, doctors, and patients, to the dizzy rapture of the discharge, the freedom of wind, sunshine, and the beautiful world. The poet to whom such an experience has come, the man, perhaps, whom such an experience has made a poet, must be accounted singularly fortunate. Of the men who rhyme, so large a number are cursed with suburban comforts. A villa and books never made a poet; they do but tend to the building up of the respectable virtues; and for the respectable virtues poetry has but the slightest use. To roam in the sun and air with vagabonds, to haunt the strange corners of cities, to know all the useless, and improper, and amusing people who are alone very much worth knowing; to live, as well as to observe life; or, to be shut up in hospital, drawn out of the rapid current of life into a sordid and exasperating inaction; to wait, for a time, in the ante-room of death: it is such things as these that make for poetry. Just as those months in prison had their influence on Verlaine, bringing out in his work a deeper note than even the passionate experiences of early life, so that hospital experience has had its influence upon Mr. Henley. The very subject, to begin with, was a discovery. Here is verse made out of personal sensations, verse which is half physiological, verse which is pathology; and yet, at its best, poetry. It is one of the modern discoveries that "the dignity of the subject" is a mere figure of speech, and a misleading one. See what Mr. Whistler can make out of "Brock's Benefit:" in place of fireworks and vulgarity you have a harmony in black and gold, and a work of art. See what Degas can discover for you in the crossing of colours, the violent rhythm of movements, the crowded and empty spaces, of a ballet rehearsal. And so, instead of prattling about Phyllis, Mr. Henley has set himself to the task of rendering the more difficult poetry of the disagreeable. And in these curious poems, the sonnets and the "rhythms," as he calls his unrhymed verse, he has etched a series of impressions which are like nothing else that I know in verse. What an odd, and, in its way, admirable triumph of remembered and recorded sensation is this picture, for instance, "The Operation":

> You are carried in a basket,
>   Like a carcass from the shambles,
>   To the theatre, a cockpit
>   Where they stretch you on a table.
>
> Then they bid you close your eyelids,
>   And they mask you with a napkin,
>   And the anæsthetic reaches
>   Hot and subtle through your being.

MODERNITY IN VERSE

And you gasp and reel and shudder
    In a rushing, swaying rapture,
    While the voices at your elbow
    Fade—receding—fainter—farther.

Lights about you shower and tumble,
    And your blood seems crystallising—
    Edged and vibrant, yet within you
    Racked and hurried back and forward.

Then the lights grow fast and furious,
    And you hear a noise of waters,
    And you wrestle, blind and dizzy,
    In an agony of effort,

Till a sudden lull accepts you,
    And you sound an utter darkness . . .
    And awaken . . . with a struggle . . .
    On a hushed, attentive audience.

And we feel, and it seems to be by a new process that we are made to feel, the long nights of lying awake, the restlessness of the tumbled bed, the sound of a leaking cistern when, "at the barren heart of midnight," it "taps upon the heartstrings:" the long days of wondering at the spring through one's prison windows, with only the change of a new patient brought in (the man who had tried to cut his throat, the man whose spine was broken) or occasionally a visitor, the "Apparition" (who, we know, was Stevenson) the "Interlude" of of a New Year's frolic among the patients. Here is verse which seems, like the violin-playing of Sarasate, to be made out of our nerves; verse which, if it almost physically hurts us, does so in common with many of our favourite renderings of the arts.

"In Hospital" gives us one side of Mr. Henley's talent, and it throws a vivid light on the conditions under which so much brave work has been done. For Mr. Henley, of all the poets of the day, is the most strenuously certain that life is worth living, the most eagerly defiant of fate, the most heroically content with death. There is, indeed, something of the spirit of Walt Whitman in his passion for living, his acceptance of the hour when man,

> Tired of experience, turns
> To the friendly and comforting breast
> Of the old nurse, Death.

His special "note," in the earlier work particularly, is a manly Bohemianism, a refreshingly reckless joy in the happy accidents of existence. Always insistently modern, with such curious use of "hansoms," of "fifth-floor windows," of bathers that "bob," of "washermaids" in the midst of "a shower of suds," he has set some of the most human of emotions to a music that is itself curiously modern.

> There is a wheel inside my head
>   Of wantonness and wine,
>   A cracked old fiddle is grunting without;
> But the wind with scents of the sea is fed,
>   And the sun seems glad to shine.
>
> The sun and the wind are akin to you,
>   As you are akin to June;
>   But the fiddle! . . . it giggles and buzzes about,
> And, love and laughter! who gave him the cue?—
>   He's playing your favourite tune.

There, is a snatch, a jingle, which, slight as one may call it, seems to me to give a particular, well-known, hardly defined sensation with ingenious success. It is a sensation which is so vague in itself, so vague and delicious, a frivolous, an inconstant, an inconsequent sensation, born of chance and happy idleness, and a pleasant and unimportant memory, that to render it requires a more genuine attack of what we call inspiration than I know not how many fine, sober-pacing sonnets, marching to order. Songs like this, and like so many of Mr. Henley's, are only possible to a rare union of a very special temperament (more often found in people who are not writers) and a very special artistic endowment. There are poets who could express everything if they could only feel anything; others who feel acutely, but can never give out in poetry what they have received in sensation. Perhaps the typical example of the latter was the late Lord Lytton. A diplomatist, a man of the world, a traveller, he was a diligent student of life, a man of many capacities, many adventures, with infinite opportunities and the keenest desire to profit by them. His personal appreciation of the human comedy was immense; his own part in it was constant, considerable, and to himself always an excitement. Yet, after all, he was never able to strike the personal note in verse: it is only from some stray suggestion that one divines the genuine emotion that has doubtless really awakened this music which he plays to us with studied fingers on a borrowed lute. A large part of contemporary verse is, of course, concerned with quite other issues, and does not even try to do what may well seem the one thing worth doing, the one thing left to be done. This, which Stevenson has done in prose, Mr. Henley has done in verse. One might call it personal romance, the romance of oneself; just what nine-tenths of the world never discover at all, even for private use. I feel a bourgeois solemnity in much of the really quite good, the very respectable work in verse that is done now-a-days; bourgeois, for all its distinction, of a kind. Our fine craftsmen are aghast at passion, afraid of emotion, ashamed of frivolity; only anxious that the sentiment as well as the rhyme should be right. It is the bourgeois, perhaps I should say the genteel, point of view: poetry from the clubs for the clubs. I am inclined to believe that no good poetry was ever written in a club armchair. Something in the air of those ponderous institutions seems to forbid the exercise of so casual a freak as verse. And with Mr. Henley it is indeed casual; casual as one's moods, sensations, caprices; casual as the only aspect of fate that we are quite certain of.

To say this is not to deny to Mr. Henley some of the deeper qualities of song. His outlook on life is joyous, in spite of misfortune; his outlook on destiny and death is grave, collected, welcoming.

> Crosses and troubles a-many have proved me.
> One or two women (God bless them!) have loved me.
> I have worked and dreamed, and I've talked at will.
> Of art and drink I have had my fill.
> I've comforted here, I've succoured there.
> I've faced my foes, and I've backed my friends.
> I've blundered, and sometimes made amends.
> I have prayed for light, and I've known despair.
> Now I look before, as I look behind,
> Come storm, come shine, whatever befall,
> With a grateful heart and a constant mind,
> For the end I know is the best of all.

There, is a sort of epilogue, or last will and testament, and it is very explicit. Prizing in life much that is merely delightful, and the charm of passing moments, what he prizes most of all is the emotion of vital deeds, the ecstasy of conflict, the passion of love, of patriotism:

> What have I done for you,
>   England, my England?
> What is there I would not do,
>   England, my own?

the vivid sense of life "at the very top of being." To quote some of his own words, it is "the beauty and the joy of living, the beauty and the blessedness of death, the glory of battle and adventure, the nobility of devotion—to a cause, an ideal, a passion even—the dignity of resistance, the sacred quality of patriotism." He is ashamed of none of the natural human instincts, and writes of women like a man, without effeminacy and without offence, content to be at one with the beneficent seasons, the will of nature. And has he not written, once and for all, the song of the soul of man in the shadow of the unknown? Such a song is the equivalent of a great deed.

> Out of the night that covers me,
>   Black as the pit from pole to pole,
> I thank whatever gods may be
>   For my unconquerable soul.
>
> In the fell clutch of circumstance
>   I have not winced nor cried aloud.
> Under the bludgeonings of chance
>   My head is bloody, but unbowed.
>
> Beyond this place of wrath and tears
>   Looms but the Horror of the shade,
> And yet the menace of the years
>   Finds and shall find me unafraid.
>
> It matters not how straight the gate,
>   How charged with punishments the scroll,
> I am the master of my fate,
>   I am the captain of my soul.

But I find myself returning to the *London Voluntaries* as perhaps the most individual, the most characteristically modern, and the most entirely successful, of Mr. Henley's work in verse. Here the subject is the finest of modern subjects, the pageant of London. Intensely personal in the feeling that transfuses the picture, it is with a brush of passionate impressionism that he paints for us the London of midsummer nights, London at "the golden end" of October afternoons, London cowering in winter under the Wind-Fiend "out of the poisonous east," London in all the ecstasy of spring. The style is freer, the choice of words, the direction of rhythms, more sure, the language more select and effectual in eloquence, than elsewhere. There is no eccentricity in rhythm, no experimentalizing, nothing tentative. There is something classical, a note (shall we say?) of *Lycidas,* in these most modern of poems, almost as if modernity had become classical. The outcome of many experiments, they have passed beyond that stage into the stage of existence.

Revolutionary always, Mr. Henley has had a wholesome but perilous discontent with the conventions of language and of verse. He is an artist who is also a critic, and the book of *Views and Reviews,* striking on its own account, has its value also in illustration of his artistic principles, preferences, and innovations. That book ("less a book," the author tells us, "than a mosaic of scraps and shreds recovered from the shot rubbish of some fourteen years of journalism") shows us an active and varied intelligence, precipitately concerned with things in general, very emphatic in likes and dislikes, never quite dispassionately, always acutely, honestly, eagerly. His characteristics of feeling and expression, and not any reasoned or prejudiced partiality, make him the champion or the foe of every writer with whom he concerns himself.

Brilliant, original, pictorial, his style tires by its pungency, dazzles by its glitter. Every word must be emphatic, every stroke must score heavily, every sentence must be an epigram or a picture or a challenge. With a preference, he tells us, for the "unobtrusive graces," for "tranquil writing," for "eloquence without adjectives," he is consistent in his negation of all these ideals of the urbane style. And, with this, immense cleverness, an acuteness that pierces and delights to pierce, an invention of phrases that is often of the essence of criticism, an extensive knowledge, extensive sympathies. His vocabulary is unusually large, and it is used, too recklessly indeed, but in a surprisingly novel, personal way. Turning to the poems, we find many of the faults of the prose, but we find also that the artist in verse is far more careful than the craftsman in prose, and that he has curbed himself to a restraint in the debauch of coloured and sounding words, still sufficiently coloured and sounding for an equally novel and personal effect. What Mr. Henley has brought into the language of poetry is a certain freshness, a daring straightforwardness and pungency of epithet, very refreshing in its contrast with the traditional limpness and timidity of the respectable verse of the day. One feels indeed at times that the touch is a little rough, the voice a trifle loud, the new word just a little unnecessary. But with these unaccustomed words and tones Mr. Henley

MODERNITY IN VERSE

does certainly succeed in flashing the picture, the impression upon us, in realizing the intangible, in saying new things in a new and fascinating manner. Here, for instance, is an impression of night and the sea, in their mood of deadly companionship:

> A desolate shore,
> The sinister seduction of the moon,
> The menace of the irreclaimable sea.
>
> Flaunting, tawdry and grim,
> From cloud to cloud along her beat,
> Leering her battered and inveterate leer,
> She signals where he prowls in the dark alone,
> Her horrible old man,
> Mumbling old oaths and warming
> His villainous old bones with villainous talk—
> The secrets of their grisly housekeeping
> Since they went out upon the pad
> In the first twilight of self-conscious Time:
> Growling, obscene and hoarse,
> Tales of unnumbered ships,
> Goodly and strong, companions of the Advance,
> In some vile alley of the night
> Waylaid and bludgeoned—
> Dead.
>
> Deep cellared in primeval ooze,
> Ruined, dishonoured, spoiled,
> They lie where the lean water-worm
> Crawls free of their secrets, and their broken sides
> Bulge with the slime of life.   Thus they abide,
> Thus fouled and desecrate,
> The summons of the Trumpet, and the while
> These Twain, their murderers,
> Unravined, imperturbable, unsubdued,
> Hang at the heels of their children—she aloft
> As in the shining streets,
> He as in ambush at some fetid stair.

> The stalwart ships,
> The beautiful and bold adventurers!
> Stationed out yonder in the isle,
> The tall Policeman,
> Flashing his bull's-eye, as he peers
> About him in the ancient vacancy,
> Tells them this way is safety—this way home.

This vigorous and most modern piece, with others of Mr. Henley's "rhythms," seems to me, in its way, so satisfying, that I sometimes wonder whether it is an unreasonable prejudice that inclines me to question the wisdom of doing without rhyme in measures that seem to demand it. The experiment has been made by Heine, by Matthew Arnold, and undoubtedly with a certain measure of success. But to do without rhyme is to do without one of the beauties of poetry, I should say one of the inherent beauties. Our ears are so accustomed to it that they have come to require it, and it is certain, for one thing, that no rhymeless lyric could become really popular, and extremely likely, for another, that an innovation which begins by dropping rhyme will end by abandoning rhythm. It has been tried in France, persistently, most ingeniously, never, I think, successfully. The example of the French Decadents should be a warning to those in England who are anxious to loosen the bonds of verse. Everything that can be done has been done; there are treatises on poetical orchestration as well as examples of it; there is a *Pélerin Passionné* and its little fame to boast of. Yet the really great, the really modern poet of France has always held aloof from these extravagances, and he has given his opinion very frankly on those young *confrères* who reproach him " with having kept a metre, and in this metre some cæsura, and rhymes at the end of the lines. *Mon Dieu!* " he adds, " I thought I had ' broken ' verse quite sufficiently." Yet, supposing even that one admits the legitimacy of the experiment, is not the inexpediency of it somewhat strongly indicated by the deeper impressiveness, the more certain mastery of the *London Voluntaries* which are rhymed ? There, surely, is Mr. Henley's most satisfactory work, his entirely characteristic rendering of modern subjects in appropriate form. A new subject, an individual treatment, a form which retains all that is helpful in tradition, while admitting all that is valuable in experiment ; that, I think, is modernity becoming classical.

A NOTE ON ZOLA'S METHOD

The art of Zola is based on certain theories, a view of humanity which he has adopted as his formula. As a deduction from his formula, he takes many things in human nature for granted, he is content to observe at second-hand; and it is only when he comes to the filling-up of his outlines, the *mise-en-scène*, that his observation becomes personal, minute, and persistent. He has thus succeeded in being at once unreal where reality is most essential, and tediously real where a point by point reality is sometimes unimportant. The contradiction is an ingenious one, which it may be interesting to examine in a little detail, and from several points of view.

And, first of all, take *L'Assommoir*, no doubt the most characteristic of Zola's novels, and probably the best; and, leaving out for the present the broader question of his general conception of humanity, let us look at Zola's manner of dealing with his material, noting by the way certain differences between his manner and that of Goncourt, of Flaubert, with both of whom he has so often been compared, and with whom he wishes to challenge comparison. Contrast *L'Assommoir* with *Germinie*

Lacerteux, which, it must be remembered, was written thirteen years earlier. Goncourt, as he incessantly reminds us, was the first novelist in France to deliberately study the life of the people, after precise documents; and *Germinie Lacerteux* has this distinction, among others, that it was a new thing. And it is done with admirable skill; as a piece of writing, as a work of art, it is far superior to Zola. But, certainly, Zola's work has a mass and bulk, a *fougue*, a *portée*, which Goncourt's lacks; and it has a savour of plebeian flesh which all the delicate art of Goncourt could not evoke. Zola sickens you with it; but there it is. As in all his books, but more than in most, there is something greasy, a smear of eating and drinking; the pages, to use his own phrase, "grasses des lichades du lundi." In *Germinie Lacerteux* you never forget that Goncourt is an aristocrat; in *L'Assommoir* you never forget that Zola is a bourgeois. Whatever Goncourt touches becomes, by the mere magic of his touch, charming, a picture; Zola is totally destitute of charm. But how, in *L'Assommoir*, he drives home to you the horrid realities of these narrow, uncomfortable lives! Zola has made up his mind that he will say *everything*, without omitting a single item, whatever he has to say; thus, in *L'Assommoir*, there is a great feast which lasts for fifty pages, beginning with the picking of the goose, the day before, and going on to the picking of the goose's bones, by a stray marauding cat, the night after. And, in a sense, he does say everything; and there, certainly, is his novelty, his invention. He observes with immense persistence, but his observation, after all, is only that of the man in the street; it is simply carried into detail, deliberately. And, while Goncourt wanders away sometimes into arabesques, indulges in flourishes, so finely artistic is his sense of words and of the things they represent, so perfectly can he match a sensation or an impression by its figure in speech, Zola, on the contrary, never finds just the right word, and it is his persistent fumbling for it which produces these miles of description; four pages describing how two people went upstairs, from the ground-floor to the sixth story, and then two pages afterwards to describe how they came downstairs again. Sometimes, by his prodigious diligence and minuteness, he succeeds in giving you the impression; often, indeed; but at the cost of what *ennui* to writer and reader alike! And so much of it all is purely unnecessary, has no interest in itself and no connection with the story: the precise details of Lorilleux's chain-making, bristling with technical terms: it was *la colonne* that he made, and only that particular kind of chain; Goujet's forge, and the machinery in the shed next door; and just how you cut out zinc with a large pair of scissors. When Goncourt gives you a long description of anything, even if you do not feel that it helps on the story very much, it is such a beautiful thing in itself, his mere way of writing it is so enchanting, that you find yourself wishing it longer, at its longest. But with Zola, there is no literary interest in the writing, apart from its clear and coherent expression of a given thing; and these interminable descriptions have no extraneous, or, if you will, implicit interest, to save them from the charge of irrelevancy; they sink by their own weight. Just as Zola's vision is the vision of the average man, so his vocabulary, with all its technicology, remains mediocre, incapable of expressing subtleties, incapable of a really artistic effect. To find out in a slang dictionary that a filthy idea can be expressed by an ingeniously filthy phrase in *argot*, and to use that phrase, is not a great feat, or, on purely artistic grounds, altogether desirable. To go to a chain-maker and learn the trade name of the various kinds of chain which he manufactures, and of the instruments with which he manufactures them, is not an elaborate process, or one which can be said to pay you for the little trouble which it no doubt takes. And it is not well to be too certain after all, that Zola is always perfectly accurate in his use of all this manifold knowledge. The slang, for example; he went to books for it, in books he found it, and no one will ever find some of it but in books. However, my main contention is that Zola's general use of words is, to be quite frank, somewhat ineffectual. He tries to do what Flaubert did, without Flaubert's tools, and without the craftsman's hand at the back of the tools. His fingers are too thick; they leave a blurred line. If you want merely weight, a certain kind of force, you get it; but no more.

Where a large part of Zola's merit lies, in his persistent attention to detail, one finds also one of his crowning defects. He cannot leave well alone; he cannot omit; he will not take the most obvious fact for granted. "Il marcha le premier, elle le suivit"; well, of course she followed him, if he walked first; why mention the fact? That beginning of a sentence is absolutely typical; it is impossible for him to refer, for the twentieth time, to some unimportant character, without giving name and profession, not one or the other, but both, invariably both. He tells us particularly that a room is composed of four walls, that a table stands on its four legs. And he does not appear to see the difference between doing that and doing as Flaubert does, namely, selecting precisely the detail out of all others which renders or consorts with the scene in hand, and giving that detail with an ingenious exactness. Here, for instance, in *Madame Bovary*, is a characteristic detail in the manner of Flaubert: "Huit jours après, comme elle étendait du linge dans sa cour, elle fut prise d'un crachement de sang, el le lendemain, tandis que Charles avait le dos tourné pour fermer le rideau de la fenêtre, elle dit: 'Ah! mon Dieu!' poussa un soupir et s'évanouit. Elle était morte." Now that detail, brought in without the slightest emphasis, of the husband turning his back at the very

A NOTE ON ZOLA'S METHOD

instant that his wife dies, is a detail of immense psychological value; it indicates to us, at the very opening of the book, just the character of the man about whom we are to read so much. Zola would have taken at least two pages to say that, and, after all, he would not have said it. He would have told you the position of the chest of drawers in the room, what wood the chest of drawers was made of, and if it had a little varnish knocked off at the corner of the lower cornice, just where it would naturally be in the way of people's feet as they entered the door. He would have told you how Charles leant against the other corner of the chest of drawers, and that the edge of the upper cornice left a slight dent in his black frock-coat, which remained visible half-an-hour afterwards. But that one little detail, which Flaubert selects from among a thousand, that, no, he would never have given us that!

And the language in which all this is written, apart from the consideration of language as a medium, is really not literature at all, in any strict sense. I am not, for the moment, complaining of the colloquialism and the slang. Zola has told us that he has, in *L'Assommoir*, used the language of the people in order to render the people with a closer truth. Whether he has done that or not, is not the question. The question is, that he does not give one the sense of reading good literature, whether he speaks in Delvau's *langue verte*, or the impeccable Academy's latest edition of classical French. His sentences have no rhythm; they give no pleasure to the ear; they carry no sensation to the eye. You hear a sentence of Flaubert, and you see a sentence of Goncourt, like living things, with forms and voices. But a page of Zola lies dull and silent before you; it draws you by no charm, it has no meaning until you have read the page that goes before and the page that comes after. It is like cabinet-makers' work, solid, well fitted together, and essentially made to be used.

Yes, there is no doubt that Zola writes very badly, worse than any other French writer of eminence. It is true that Balzac, certainly one of the greatest, does, in a sense, write badly; but his way of writing badly is very different from Zola's, and leaves you with the sense of quite a different result. Balzac is too impatient with words, he cannot stay to get them all into proper order, to pick and choose among them. Night, the coffee, the wet towel, and the end of six hours' labour, are often too much for him; and his manner of writing his novels on the proof-sheets, altering and expanding as fresh ideas came to him on each re-reading, was not a way of doing things which can possibly result in perfect writing. But Balzac sins from excess, from a feverish haste, the very extravagance of power; and at all events *peccat fortiter*. Zola sins meanly, he is penuriously careful, he does the best he possibly can; and he is not aware that his best does not answer all requirements. So long as writing is clear, and not ungrammatical, it seems to him sufficient. He has not realized that without charm there can be no fine literature, as there can be no perfect flower without fragrance.

I think one may mention in the same connection, for it is not on moral grounds that I object to it, Zola's obsession by what is grossly, uninterestingly filthy. There is a certain simile in *L'Assommoir*, used in the most innocent connection, in connection with a bonnet, which seems to me the most abjectly dirty phrase which I have ever read. It is one thing to use dirty words to describe dirty things; that may be necessary, and thus unexceptionable. It is another thing again, and this, too, may well be defended on artistic grounds, to be ingeniously and wittily indecent. But I do not think a real man of letters could possibly have used such an expression as the one I am alluding to, or could so meanly succumb to certain kinds of prurience which we find in Zola's work. Such a scene as the one in which Gervaise comes home with Lantier, and finds her husband lying drunk asleep in his own vomit, might certainly be explained, and even excused, though few more disagreeable things were ever written, on the ground of the psychological importance which it undoubtedly has, and the overwhelming way in which it drives home the point which it is the writer's business to make. But the worrying way in which *la derrière* and *le ventre* are constantly kept in view, without the slightest necessity, is quite another thing. I should not like to say how often the phrase "sa nudité de jolie fille" occurs in Zola. Zola's nudities always remind me of those which you can see in the Foire au pain d'épice at Vincennes, by paying a penny and looking through a peep-hole. In the laundry scenes, for instance, in *L'Assommoir*, he is always reminding you that the laundresses have turned up their sleeves, or undone a button or two of their bodices. His eyes seem eternally fixed on the inch or two of bare flesh that can be seen; and he nudges your elbow at every moment, to make sure that you are looking too. Nothing is more charming than a frankly sensuous description of things which appeal to the senses; but can one imagine anything less charming, less like art, than this prying eye glued to the peep-hole in the Gingerbread Fair?

Yet, whatever view may be taken of Zola's work in literature, there is no doubt that the life of Zola is a model lesson, and might profitably be told in one of Dr. Smiles's edifying biographies. It may even be brought as a reproach against the writer of these novels, in which there are so many offences against the respectable virtues, that he is too good a bourgeois, too much the incarnation of the respectable virtues, to be a man of genius. If the finest art comes of the intensest living, then Zola has never had even a chance of doing the greatest kind of work. It is his merit and his misfortune to have lived entirely in and for his books, with a heroic devotion to his ideal of literary duty which would merit every praise if we had to consider simply the moral side of the question. So many pages of copy a day, so many hours of study given to mysticism, or Les Halles ; Zola has always had his day's work marked out before him, and he has never swerved from it. A recent life of Zola tells us something about his way of getting up a subject. " Immense preparation had been necessary for the *Faute de l'Abbé Mouret*. Mountains of note-books were heaped up on his table, and for months Zola was plunged in the study of religious works. All the mystical part of the book, and notably the passages having reference to the cultus of Mary, was taken from the works of the Spanish Jesuits. The *Imitation of Jesus Christ* was largely drawn upon, many passages being copied almost word for word into the novel—much as in *Clarissa Harlowe*, that other great realist, Richardson, copied whole passages from the Psalms. The description of life in a grand seminary was given him by a priest who had been dismissed from ecclesiastical service. The little church of Sainte Marie des Batignolles was regularly visited."

How commendable all that is, but, surely, how futile! Can one conceive of a more hopeless, a more ridiculous task, than that of setting to work on a novel of ecclesiastical life as if one were cramming for an examination in religious knowledge ? Zola apparently imagines that he can master mysticism in a fortnight, as he masters the police regulations of Les Halles. It must be admitted that he does wonders with his second-hand information, alike in regard to mysticism and Les Halles. But he succeeds only to a certain point, and that point lies on the nearer side of what is really meant by success. Is not Zola himself, at his moments, aware of this? A letter written in 1881, and printed in Mr. Sherard's life of Zola, from which I have just quoted, seems to me very significant.

"I continue to work in a good state of mental equilibrium. My novel (*Pot-Bouille*) is certainly only a task requiring precision and clearness. No *bravoura*, not the least lyrical treat. It does not give me any warm satisfaction, but it amuses me like a piece of mechanism with a thousand wheels, of which it is my duty to regulate the movements with the most minute care. I ask myself the question: Is it good policy, when one feels that one has passion in one, to check it, or even to bridle it? If one of my books is destined to become immortal, it will, I am sure, be the most passionate one."

"Est-elle en marbre ou non, la Vénus de Milo?" said the Parnassians, priding themselves on their muse with her "peplum bien sculpté." Zola will describe to you the exact shape and the exact smell of the rags of his Naturalistic muse; but has she, under the tatters, really a human heart? In the whole of Zola's works, amid all his exact and impressive descriptions of misery, all his endless annals of the poor, I know only one episode which brings tears to the eyes, the episode of the child-martyr Lalie in *L'Assommoir*. "A piece of mechanism with a thousand wheels," that is indeed the image of this immense and wonderful study of human life, evolved out of the brain of a solitary student, who knows life only by the report of his documents, his friends, and, above all, his formula.

Zola has defined art, very aptly, as nature seen through a temperament. The art of Zola is nature seen through a formula. This professed realist is a man of theories, who studies life with a conviction that he will find there such and such things, which he has read about in scientific books. He observes, indeed, with astonishing minuteness, but he observes in support of preconceived ideas. And so powerful is his imagination that he has created a whole world which has no existence anywhere but in his own brain, and he has placed there imaginary beings, so much more logical than life, in the midst of surroundings which are themselves so real as to lend almost a semblance of reality to the embodied formulas who inhabit them.

It is the boast of Zola that he has taken up art at the point where Flaubert left it, and that he has developed that art in its logical sequence. But the art of Flaubert, itself a development from Balzac, had carried realism, if not in *Madame Bovary*, at all events in *L'Education Sentimentale*, as far as realism can well go without ceasing to be art. In the grey and somewhat sordid history of Frédéric Moreau there is not a touch of romanticism, not so much as a concession to style, a momentary escape of the imprisoned lyrical tendency. Everything is observed, everything is taken straight from life: realism, sincere, direct, implacable, reigns from end to end of the book. But with what consummate art all this mass of observation is disintegrated, arranged, composed! with what infinite delicacy it is manipulated in the service of an unerring sense of construction! And Flaubert has no theory, has no prejudices, has only a certain impatience with human imbecility. Zola, too, gathers his documents, heaps up his mass of observation, and then, in this unhappy "development" of the principles of art which produced *L'Education Sentimentale*, flings everything pell-mell into one overflowing *pot-au-feu*. The probabilities of nature and the delicacies of art are alike drowned beneath a flood of turbid observation, and in the end one does not even feel convinced that Zola really knows his subject. I remember once hearing M. Huysmans, with his look and tone of subtle, ironical malice, describe how Zola, when he was writing *La Terre*, took a drive into the country in a victoria, to see the peasants. The English papers once reported an interview in which the author of *Nana*, indiscreetly questioned as to the amount of personal observation he had put into the book, replied that he had lunched with an actress of the Variétés. The reply was generally taken for a joke, but the lunch was a reality, and it was assuredly a rare experience in the life of solitary diligence to which we owe so many impersonal studies in life. Nor did Zola, as he sat silent by the side of Mlle. X., seem to be making much use of the opportunity. The language of the miners in *Germinal*, how much of local colour is there in that? The interminable additions and divisions, the extracts from a financial gazette, in *L'Argent*, how much of the real temper and idiosyncrasy of the financier do they give us? In his description of places, in his *mise-en-scène*, Zola puts down what he sees with his own eyes, and, though it is often done at utterly disproportionate length, it is at all events done with exactitude. But in the far more important observation of men and women, he is content with second-hand knowledge, the knowledge of a man who sees the world through a formula. Zola sees in humanity *la bête humaine*. He sees the beast in all its transformations, but he sees only the beast. He has never looked at life impartially, he has never seen it as it is. His realism is a distorted idealism, and the man who considers himself the first to paint humanity as it really is, will be remembered in the future as the most idealistic writer of his time.

III NOTES AND IMPRESSIONS

I ENGLISH WRITERS

RICHARD JEFFERIES

THE early books of Richard Jefferies, those by which he won his fame, those, no doubt, on which his fame will rest, *The Gamekeeper at Home* and its immediate successors, owe but little of their charm to purely literary merits; they may almost be said to owe their charm to the very absence of the literary element. They are bundles of jottings, notes taken direct from life in a reporter's note-book, observations recorded because they are observed, and in just the words in which they presented themselves, hasty impressions of life on the wing, impressions slowly imbibed and lengthily developed, scrapes and samples picked and sorted and placed or thrown together, with little more of artistic adjustment than Nature herself expends on her heterogeneous collection of exhibits. Quickness of eye and faithfulness of hand are his two great qualities, as shown in these early books; and it is, I think, in the impression of absolute veracity, not coloured with prepossessions, not distorted by an artistic presentment, that he has the advantage over Thoreau, so much his superior as a writer; over Mr. Thomas Hardy, who "places" his rural pictures; over everybody, indeed, except in the purely naturalist section, Gilbert White. These books are, both literally, and in the impression they convey, the work of a man who has grown up on a farm, who has lived in the open air, wandering in the fields and woods from morning till night with a gun across his shoulder, looking at everything with a free and open interest, and forgetting nothing. He is not a poet who comes to Nature with a pantheist rapture, and yearns so strongly for her spirit that he goes at least quite through her outward form; nor a painter who values Nature for her lines and colours, her admirable suggestions for a work of art. He is content to see no more, he will be content with seeing no less, than the gamekeeper or the ploughboy sees without regarding: fields, and animals, and birds, just as they are in themselves. He will see (and everything that he sees he will remember, for memory is merely the crystallization of intense interest) all that the sharpest, the most sympathetic observation can show him: what began instinctively, the habit of observing, will be followed up by set purpose, and so perseveringly, that he will think nothing of walking along a certain road daily, during a whole spring or summer, so that he may gain a thorough knowledge of the habits of the birds which frequent it. Consequently, there is hardly anything in "the life of the fields" that he has not seen or described; and to read those early books of his, must, to the town-dweller, be almost the equivalent of an actual walk in the country.

Such books as these must be valued for their

exhilarating qualities: so few even of the best books freshen a jaded sense, or help to brighten our dull outlook on things! Jefferies brought the fields nearer London; he admitted the dingy folk of cities to the most select society of country nature. He made them the intimates of the birds and animals, whom indeed he knew better than his fellow-men. To those who know the country well there will be little actually novel in Jefferies' sketches; he writes almost wholly of things that one must have seen many times: things so familiar that our notions of them are blurred and hazy, like our notions of the wall-paper of a familiar room. Here we see them all in black and white; and with all their details, which perhaps we never knew, or have forgotten. I have said that Jefferies knew the birds and animals better than his fellow-men. I think this may be emphasized. In *Hodge and his Masters* there are many clever sketches of village life, and they are generally true as far as they go; but set a chapter on the habits of birds against a chapter on the habits of men, and how much more insight you will find in the former than the latter! Jefferies will give you the flora and fauna of the village with incomparable accuracy; but for the villager, go to Mr. Hardy or Dr. Jessop.

This lack of human interest, and the knowledge which is the fruit of interest, told heavily on Jefferies when, towards the close of his life, he tried to become a novelist. In his novels (*Greene Ferne*

Farm, The Dewy Morn, Amaryllis at the Fair, such delightful names as they have!) we meet with passages as full of charm as anything he ever wrote; but they are passages that have little to do with the story; and it is hard to see why he should have strung together a plot whose only use is that it serves to introduce these passages, which would unquestionably be better without it. One book, which in a certain sense is a story, must be excepted from this category: the fresh and delightful apologue or fairy-tale named *Wood-Magic*. Here, with a truer instinct, he has taken for his *dramatis personæ* Kapchack the magpie, Choo-hoo the wood-pigeon, La Schach the pretty jay, and of humankind only a little boy, Sir Bevis, who knows the language of the birds and creatures, and to whom they will talk as if he were one of themselves. The sequel to *Wood-Magic*, *Bevis*, though an interesting tale enough, sinks to the ordinary level of boys' books of adventure: it has some good fighting, and the inevitable desert island.

But though some of Jefferies' later books are disappointing, and seem to have been manufactured for a public, there are one or two which have a special, though in some cases a divided interest, and show the development of an almost unsuspected side of his nature. In the *Gamekeeper* and its companions there is little of the literary element, little form, little instinct of the pictorial except as an accident of nature: these negative qualities are, as I have said, in their way merits, for their absence gives us something which their presence could not give. Still, there is the lack; and by-and-by, as the freshness wore off his recollections and his pen began to drag, Jefferies discovered it, and, what is more wonderful, he supplied it. It was not always a satisfactory substitute, people thought, for what was lost: but there it was, unmistakable, a style, an attitude, a literary quality.

This new tendency, new as to its manifestation in his work, was the outcome of a passionate love of beauty, perhaps only another phase of that vivid interest in country life which inspired his earlier books. Doubtless it was latent from the first, but there is not a sentence indicating it in *The Gamekeeper at Home*, and only occasional signs of it in the *Wild Life in a Southern County*. Here we have the naturalist, the observer without *arrière pensée*, the genuine countryman pursuing the picturesque with a gun. Take this sentence, for instance, from the *Gamekeeper*: "Once on a hawthorn branch in a hedge I saw a mouse descending with an acorn; he was, perhaps, five feet from the ground, and how and from whence he had got his burden was rather puzzling at first." Here the interest is in the thing itself, there is no attempt at painting a picture or making an impression, but simply at describing a curious circumstance which has been observed. Now turn to this sentence which I take from "Golden-Brown," one of the chapters in the book called *The Open Air*: "Green foliage overhung them and the men with whom they were drinking; the white pipes, the blue smoke, the flash of a match, the red sign which had so often swung to and fro in the gales now still in the summer eve, the rude seats and blocks, the reaping-hooks bound about the edge with hay, the white dogs creeping from knee to knee, some such touches gave an interest to the scene." Here the thing in itself is of no interest; it is but a company of drunken men and women outside a village pothouse; but see how cunningly it is taken, how the touches of colour, making a picture of this piece of vulgar reality, are noticed and brought out, just as a painter would bring them out on his canvas. The straightforward observer has become an impressionist, he values Nature now for her suggestions. Thus he will write a brilliant piece of special-pleading to prove that Paris is "the plainest city of Europe;" another, a perfect triumph of the artistic spirit and of literary expression, to prove that the picturesqueness of Venice is nothing to the picturesqueness of the docks at the East End. There is no longer an interest in ships as ships, or in Paris for what it is rather than what it looks, or in the drunken labourers because they are drunken, and not good to have on a farm; a delight in beauty of whatever sort, of picturesqueness or the incentive to picturesqueness, has dominated every other sense. The lazy pleasantness of language which made the earlier books so easy to read has given place to a pungent, original style, not without traces of affectation at times, but full of novel felicities, sharp, precise, coloured, above all, as I said, pungent.

And now that curious lack of interest in men and women, which seemed always to leave a certain gap in the rural landscape, becomes supplied, in turn, by a sensuous and physical interest, the interest of the body and of bodily beauty. To Jefferies men and women were animals; and he adores these beautiful animals, looking on them for their grace and strength and health, for their lines and contour, with a frank materialism which flowers into poetry. There is still no sense of companionship, no intimacy or communion of spirit, none of that human curiosity which was the very keynote of George Borrow, which Robert Louis Stevenson has felt so keenly and rendered with so insinuating an enthusiasm. But the delight in physical beauty, which is one phase only of the larger feeling, this he has to the full, and it inspires some wonderful pages. His rapture over some tiny process, some unregarded corner of Nature's handiwork (the articulation of the knee-joint, for instance: who before Jefferies ever saw anything in a knee?) his phraseology, part lyrical, part technical of the physiologist, may indeed have its amusing side; and if I remember, there was grave objection on the part of the critics to some bold analogy (it was in one of his novels, and the heroine was taking a walk) used to express the expansion and contraction of the chest in walking. But there was a poetry for him in these things, and the intense sincerity of his worship of Nature is proved by his devotion to the subordinate details of her workmanship.

Jefferies started, as we have seen, with serene and quiet transcripts of the country life about him. Serenity is a quality that life is quick to abrade with its constant, uneasy friction; and the serenity wore off from Jefferies' spirit. He became an unquiet thinker, a dreamer, restless, *tourmenté*; the mind sharpened itself on the ravaged body. In this he was typical of our time, which breeds the frail intelligences it cannot satisfy nor support. His outlook on Nature through a closed window, his sick-chamber meditations on the exultant joys of health, his physical delight and satisfaction while the physical powers ebbed from him, all stamp him a child of the delicate and nervous nineteenth century. In his early blitheness he was of another age, or he played a rare pastoral delicately in ours. But the age which is not of pastorals conquered.

JAMES THOMSON

THE collected edition of James Thomson's poetical works, issued in 1894 by Messrs. Reeves and Turner, affords an opportunity, which has long been wanting, of considering in its entirety the scattered and partly lost work of a remarkable writer, who, for a short time, towards the close of an unfortunate existence, won something like real fame. The author of *The City of Dreadful Night* had to wait long for recognition; but it cannot be said that he failed, before the end, to receive at least the recognition which was his due. Of late his name has almost dropped out of sight; the critics of the hour have been too busy discussing the immortals of the moment. Yet here we have a considerable body of work, work which certainly aims at great things, work planned on a large scale, and carried out with an unquestionable force; work, too, which has been praised by those whose praise is scrupulous and weighty. How far does the work, looked at to-day, seem to justify the neglect of yesterday, or the appreciation of the day before yesterday?

It is a difficult question to answer, even to

oneself. There is that about Thomson's work which is at all events interesting; it has a human appeal, almost like that of a distressed face, seen in passing, in the street. Incorrect, commonplace, slovenly, as it so frequently is, there is a certain breath of life in it; there is, too, an unusual quality of mind, unusual in a poet, at work behind all these tawdry and slipshod lines. It has not the vice of so much correct and scholarly writing which passes for literature, and is, indeed, "literature," in the sense of Verlaine's scornful ejaculation: "Et tout le reste est littérature!" Good writing or bad writing, it is not mere writing. The circumstances of James Thomson's life are known; that "long defeat," in which love, and fame, and health, and faith, all deserting him, left him to the sordid misery of a garret in the dingiest quarter of London, with only the resources of drink and drugs, and the inevitable ending in the hospital. His work is the story of his own life, with its momentary jollities (as in "Sunday up the River") its customary gloom (as in *The City of Dreadful Night*) and that strange, occasional mingling of tragedy and comedy in a fantastic transformation of reality (as in *Vane's Story*). It was not merely circumstances that made Thomson miserable; it is difficult to imagine a temperament such as his being anything else. His extreme sense of sin, which he tried to silence by blaspheming, would have done credit to the most devout Puritan. He was always, in his own despite, and to his own despair, a moralist; and his Hyde Park atheism is only the counterpart of the Hyde Park salvationist. He is incessantly concerned with spiritual problems, with the order of the universe and with his individual peace of mind; and it is to escape from his own mental tortures that he cries aloud.

> Because a cold rage seizes one at whiles
> To show the bitter, old, and wrinkled truth
> Stripped naked of all vesture that beguiles,
> False dreams, false hopes, false masks and modes of youth;
> Because it gives some sense of power and passion
> In helpless impotence to try to fashion
> Our woe in living words howe'er uncouth.

And so the burden of his main poem is one of

> Infections of unutterable sadness,
> Infections of incalculable madness,
> Infections of incurable despair.

This tragic pessimism, so obviously and rootedly sincere, is as much a matter of temperament, demanding as purely pathological an explanation, as the inherited craving for drink which ruined the man's body. It is in this "anatomy of melancholy," in which he is generally engaged, that we see what was most intimate in Thomson; it is here, really, that he is at his best, despite the brilliance and novelty of some of his lighter work in livelier manners.

Among this lighter work there is much that demands consideration in any view of Thomson as a poet. He was ahead of the fashion in aiming at what we now call modernity; his work is, in a certain sense, more modern than that of any other considerable writer in verse. But in regard to his actual success in so difficult an endeavour, it is not quite easy to define the precise measure of attainment. The great problem presented itself to him, as it does to every writer: how to be real, true to life, and yet poetic, true to art. Thomson never quite mastered the problem: how few have ever mastered it! More than most, he cared for the trivial details, the casual accidents, of "Sundays out," and shop-girls' dancing-halls; and he tried to get the full value out of these things by a certain crudity in his transference of them to the canvas. To render vulgar life, it seemed to him necessary to be vulgar. It was in this that he made his radical misapprehension. Here is Mr. Frith with his "Derby Day," as modern as you please, but with only the commonness, the photographed surface, of things about us. For the real modernity we must turn to Degas; we find it in the new employment of a masterly and really classic art in the interpretation of just such actual things: the very race-horses, if you will, but how differently seen, and with what careful and expressive subtlety rendered! Thomson did much: he at all events caught the life at the moment of its movement; he was intensely vivid, amusing, and true to the lesser and more obvious truths of Nature. But he did not realize that to be modern is of all achievements the most difficult, that it requires the most perfect command of oneself and one's material, consummate art; and that here, more than elsewhere, a flaw, a lapse, is fatal alike to the illusion and to the distinction of success.

Thomson's poetic style, though it has breadth and at times dignity, and is almost always both impressive and incisive, is never, even in his most serious work, really finished. There is always thought at the back of it, but, when it seems to him that he has expressed his thought clearly and trenchantly, it does not occur to him that the process is not ended; he does not labour, as the true artist labours, to find the one, perfect, final expression of that thought. Surely of all subjects likely to move him to fine utterance, the subject of Heine should have been the most certain. Yet, in *Vane's Story*, he can write:

> Our poor Saint Heinrich! for he was
> A saint here of the loftiest class.

He will begin a striking poem, "To Our Ladies of Death," with this simple and powerful stanza:

> Weary of erring in this desert Life,
>   Weary of hoping hopes for ever vain,
> Weary of struggling in all-sterile strife,
>   Weary of thought which maketh nothing plain,
> I close my eyes and calm my panting breath,
> And pray to Thee, O ever-quiet Death!
>   To come and soothe away my bitter pain.

And then, a few stanzas further on, he will slip unconsciously into false and pompous commonplace such as:

> Infatuate in a Siren's weird embrace.

He can be grandiose, and with real effect, and next moment merely turgid. At his best in such large movements as the three polysyllabic lines I have quoted from *The City of Dreadful Night*, he is rarely without a suspicion of commonness, which slips out, like a vulgarism in speech, at just the crucial moment. He formed his style, one would say, laboriously; it appears to be the result of much study, and the study of many models, of whom the chief were Shelley, Browning, and Heine. It was probably from Shelley that he acquired his fondness for vague symbolism; from Browning that he learnt a certain trick of writing verse in almost the same key as prose; from Heine that he copied, not always successfully, a manner of executing discords with intention. Out of these varying styles he built up a style which he made individual, indeed, but with an individuality which, above all things, lacked distinction. Contrast, for instance, *Vane's Story* with an equally modern poem in the same metre, Rossetti's "Jenny." Here we see at once the difference between a perfectly finished work of art and an exceedingly clever and interesting impromptu. Carelessness or incapacity, it matters not: poetic work which is not perfectly finished can never really prove satisfying, and in Thomson's very best work there is always something not quite satisfying. Yet how many qualities of almost the first order went to the making of what we cannot justly call a success! And there is always that personal interest, which, associated as it is with the pathos of Thomson's career, will perhaps do more than anything else to preserve his work from oblivion.

THOMAS GORDON HAKE

The death of Dr. Gordon Hake, at the age of eighty-six, seemed, for a moment, to draw a little attention to the fact that a remarkable poet had been living and writing in our midst, almost unrecognized. It is true that the qualities of Dr. Hake's work were, from the first, fully admitted, and warmly praised, by one of the greatest of contemporary poets, who was also a critic of exceptional acuteness, Rossetti. Indeed, the only two review-articles which Rossetti ever wrote were written on two of Dr. Hake's books: *Madeline*, which he reviewed in the *Academy* in 1871, and *Parables and Tales* which he reviewed in the *Fortnightly Review* in 1873. But to the general public, even to the cultured public, the name of Dr. Hake has been hardly even a name. The volume of selections from his poems, so carefully edited by Mrs. Meynell, seems to have made little impression on the mass of critics or of readers; and only the accident of death could at last give a certain slight actuality to a writer who had many claims on the attention of a "fit audience."

No doubt Dr. Hake could never have been a popular poet; and failing, as he did, of actual greatness, it was not his to conquer admiration by force. But he had so many singular and interesting qualities; he did, long ago, almost perfectly, so many things which younger writers have since been admired for doing imperfectly; he appealed, or should have appealed, so strongly to that modern love of the unusual, the fantastic, the morbid, that it is surprising he should never have had so much as a little inner circle of disciples. For how long has it not been the fashion to admire whatever is exotic! Well, never was an English poet more exotic than Dr. Hake. But no doubt the interest of his poetry is too exclusively intellectual, and concerned in too abstract a way with what Mr. Swinburne calls the "soul of sense." He goes straight to the essence of things, and the essential is always a little meagre and unsatisfying to the broad, general taste. In his first manner, it is true, the manner of the "Parables and Tales," there was a Wordsworthian homeliness, and a quaintness more resembling that of George Herbert, which might have had a certain success, if the subject-matter had been less odd and disconcerting. But with the succeeding volumes, *New Symbols*, *Legends of the Morrow*, *Maiden Ecstasy*, a new manner comes into his work, a subtle, packed, remote, deliberately and precisely vague, style which corresponds more and more closely with the ever vaguer and more remote quality of the subject. At first, in a peculiar way, certainly, a realist, at least so far as outward details are concerned, he loses all interest in the reality of what is external. A new order of phenomena absorbs his attention, which becomes more and more internalized, more exclusively concerned with the phenomena of the soul, of morbid sensation, of the curiosities of the mind and the senses. Humanity is now apprehended in a more than ever generalized, and yet specialized, way, in its essence, where it becomes, if you will, an abstraction; or, if you will, for the first time purely individual. He is now, in the true sense of one of his own titles, a "Soul-Painter."

This attitude of mind, this manner of writing, the peculiar technique of the verse, with its invariable andante movement, its lingering subtleties of sound, colour, and suggestion, the almost medical curiosity of these researches into the stuff of dreams, the very fibre of life itself, combined, certainly, to produce a new thing in poetry. The result is not an invariable success. Dr. Hake was not always entirely the master of his own enchantments. But, at his best, in such poems as "The Snake-Charmer," "The Dancing-Girl," we find an effect of extraordinary difficulty realized with extraordinary mastery.

One thing, and one thing alone, is attempted: the rendering of a certain sensation or series of sensations, a certain chain of movement, a certain philosophical idea. Not a word is to be admitted by accident, however happy, not a rhythm is to be allowed to flow freely, at its natural will; here is the effect to be rendered, and with the utmost economy of means, the utmost intensity of expression. Such a way of working (the extreme opposite to that of the spontaneous lyrical poet, to whom song is a natural outflow) naturally produces at times a sense of constraint, an actual awkwardness, which a more facile, or a more spontaneous, or a more easily contented, verse-writer would have avoided. And the attempt is sometimes after the unrealizable, a brave attempt, but one which a truer sense of the just limits of art would have prevented a fine artist from making. But how interesting, at the very least, are these sometimes foiled endeavours! It is a new kind of poetry, in which science becomes an instrument in the creation of a new, curious kind of beauty, the poetry, one might almost say, of pathology. Much of the best modern poetry, much in Baudelaire, in Poe, in Rossetti, in Mr. Swinburne's earlier work, has a certain pathological quality, which comes, partly indeed from an æsthetic fascination in what is diseased, but also largely from a purely personal, a personally unhealthy, disposition of mind. Now, in Dr. Hake, this disposition of mind is entirely absent. Dealing by preference with morbid themes, he impresses one as being himself no more morbid than the surgeon whom we see eagerly entering a hospital. The curiosity is impersonal, a study, an outside mental interest. And for this very reason it can be woven deliberately into the stuff of poetry, where its effect will have the strangest and most instructive differences from the effect of the same thing done by one who is himself really a patient.

For what he has done, and still more for what he has attempted, Dr. Hake will remain, in the estimation of those who have any real apprehension of such matters, one of the most interesting poets of our time. He did much of really fine quality, he wrote at least a few poems which deserve to live. But perhaps his special interest in the future will be that he has opened up new possibilities to poetry, that he has at least indicated the way to do certain things which no one had ever attempted to do before.

ROBERT LOUIS STEVENSON

THE death of Robert Louis Stevenson deprived English literature of the most charming and sympathetic writer of the present day. He was a fastidious craftsman, caring, we might almost say pre-eminently, for style; yet he was popular. He was most widely known as the writer of boys' books of adventure; yet he was the favourite reading of those who care only for the most literary aspects of literature. Within a few days after the news of his death reached England, English newspapers vied with each other in comparing him with Montaigne, with Lamb, with Scott, with Defoe; and he has been not merely compared, but preferred. Uncritical praise is the most unfriendly service a man can render to his friend; but here, where so much praise is due, may one not try to examine a little closely just what those qualities are which call for praise, and just what measure of praise they seem to call for?

Stevenson somewhere describes certain of his own essays as being " but the readings of a literary vagrant." And, in truth, he was always that, a literary vagrant; it is the secret of much of his charm, and much of his weakness. He wandered, a literary vagrant, over the world, across life, and across literature, an adventurous figure, with all the irresponsible and irresistible charm of the vagabond. To read him is to be for ever setting out on a fresh journey, along a white, beckoning road, on a blithe spring morning. Anything may happen, or nothing; the air is full of the gaiety of possible chances. And in this exhilaration of the blood, unreasoning, unreasonable, as it is, all the philosophies merge themselves into those two narrow lines which the *Child's Garden of Verses* piously encloses for us :

> The world is so full of a number of things,
> I am sure we should all be as happy as kings.

It is the holiday mood of life that Stevenson expresses, and no one has ever expressed it with a happier abandonment to the charm of natural things. In its exquisite exaggeration, it is the optimism of the invalid, due to his painful consciousness that health, and the delights of health, are what really matter in life. Most of those who have written captivatingly of the open air, of what are called natural, healthy things, have been invalids: Thoreau, Richard Jefferies, Stevenson. The strong man has leisure to occupy his thoughts with other things; he can indulge in abstract thinking without a twinge of the brain, can pursue the moral issues of conduct impersonally; he is not condemned to the bare elements of existence. And, in his calm acceptance of the privileges of ordinary health, he finds no place for that lyric rapture of thanksgiving which a bright day, a restful night, wakens in the invalid. The actual fever and languor in the blood: that counts for something in Stevenson's work, and lies at the root of some of its fascination.

His art, in all those essays and extravagant tales into which he put his real self, is a romantic art, alike in the essay on "Walking Tours" and the "Story of the Young Man with the Cream Tarts." Stevenson was passionately interested in people; but there was something a trifle elvish and uncanny about him, as of a bewitched being who was not actually human, had not actually a human soul, and whose keen interest in the fortunes of his fellows was really a vivid curiosity, from one not quite of the same nature as those about him. He saw life as the most absorbing, the most amusing, game; or, as a masquerade, in which he liked to glance behind a mask, now and again, on the winding and coloured way he made for himself through the midst of the pageant. It was only in his latest period that he came to think about truth to human nature; and even then it was with the picturesqueness of character, with its adaptability to the humorous freaks of incident, that he was chiefly concerned.

He was never really himself save when he was in some fantastic disguise. From "The

Pavilion on the Links" to *Dr. Jekyll and Mr. Hyde*, he played with men and women as a child plays with a kaleidoscope; using them freakishly, wantonly, as colours, sometimes as symbols. In some wonderful, artificial way, like a wizard who raises, not living men from the dead, but the shadows of men who had once died, he calls up certain terrifying, but not ungracious, phantoms, who frisk it among the mere beings of flesh and blood, bringing with them the strangest "airs from heaven or blasts from hell." No; in the phrase of Beddoes, Stevenson was "tired of being merely human." Thus there are no women in his books, no lovers; only the lure of hidden treasures and the passion of adventure. It was for the accidents and curiosities of life that he cared, for life as a strange picture, for its fortunate confusions, its whimsical distresses, its unlikely strokes of luck, its cruelties, sometimes, and the touch of madness that comes into it at moments. For reality, for the endeavour to see things as they are, to represent them as they are, he had an impatient disregard. These matters did not interest him.

But it is by style, largely, we are told, that Stevenson is to live, and the names of Lamb and of Montaigne are called up on equal terms. Style, with Stevenson, was certainly a constant preoccupation, and he has told us how, as a lad, he trained himself in the use of language; how, in his significant phrase, he "lived with words;" by "playing the sedulous ape to Hazlitt, to Lamb, to Wordsworth, to Sir Thomas Browne, to Defoe, to Hawthorne, to Montaigne, to Baudelaire, and to Obermann." He was resolved from the first to reject the ready-made in language, to combine words for himself, as if no one had ever used them before; and, with labour and luck, he formed for his use a singularly engaging manner of writing, full of charm, freshness, and flexibility, and with a certain human warmth in the words. But it is impossible to consider style in the abstract without taking into account also what it expresses; for true style is not the dress, but the very flesh, of the informing thought. Stevenson's tendency, like that of his admirers, was rather to the forgetfulness of this plain and sometimes uncongenial fact. But, in comparing him with the great names of literature, we cannot but feel all the difference, and all the meaning of the difference, between a great intellect and a bright intelligence. The lofty and familiar homeliness of Montaigne, the subtle and tragic humour of Lamb, are both on a far higher plane than the gentle and attractive and whimsical confidences of Stevenson. And, underlying what may seem trifling in both, there is a large intellectual force, a breadth of wisdom, which makes these two charming writers not merely charming, but great. Stevenson remains charming; his personality, individual and exquisite as it was, had not the strength and depth of greatness. And, such as it was, it gave itself to us completely; there was no sense, as there is with the really great writers, of reserve power, of infinite riches to draw upon. Quite by himself in a certain seductiveness of manner, he ranks, really, with Borrow and Thoreau, with the men of secondary order in literature, who appeal to us with more instinctive fascination than the very greatest; as a certain wayward and gipsy grace in a woman thrills to the blood, often enough, more intimately and immediately than the august perfection of classic beauty. He is one of those writers who speak to us on easy terms, with whom we may exchange affections. We cannot lose our heart to Shakespeare, to Balzac; nay, even to Montaigne, because of the height and depth, the ardour and dignity, of the wisdom in his " smiling pages " (to use Stevenson's own word). But George Borrow makes every one who comes under his charm a little unfit for civilization, a little discontented with drawing-rooms; Thoreau leads his willing victim into the ardent austerity of the woods; and Stevenson awakens something of the eternal romance in the bosom even of the conventional. It is a surprising, a marvellous thing to have done; and to afford such delights, to call forth such responsive emotions, is a boon that we accept with warmer rejoicing than many more solid gifts. But to be wine and song to us for a festive evening is, after all, not the highest form of service or the noblest ministration of joy. It is needful to discrimiuate in these generous and perilous enthusiasms, as it is in judging fairly of the character of a friend. Let us love our friend, with all his shortcomings; let him be the more lovable for them, if chance wills it; but it is better to be aware of the truth, before we proceed to act with affectionate disregard of it. Stevenson captivates the heart: that is why he is in such danger of being wronged by indiscriminate eulogy. Let us do him justice: he would have wished only for justice. It is a dishonour to the dead if we strive to honour their memory with anything less absolute than truth.

JOHN ADDINGTON SYMONDS

Mr. Horatio Brown's Life of John Addington Symonds is composed with so careful and so successful a reticence on the part of the author, that it is not at first sight obvious how much its concealment of art is a conscious subtlety in art. These two volumes, containing, for the most part, extracts from an autobiography, from diaries and from letters, woven together so as to make an almost consecutive narrative (a plan which recalls a little the admirable and unusual method of Mason's *Gray*) present a most carefully arranged portrait, which, in one sense, is absolutely the creation of the biographer. All this material, ready-made as it may seem to be, has really been fitted together, according to a well-defined scheme, with immense ingenuity and diligence, and, with a remarkable subtlety and insight into the very complex nature of the man whose portrait is here presented to the world. It is a painful, a tragic book, this record of what Symonds calls "my chequered, confused, and morally perturbed existence," and yet at the same time an inspiring, an exhilarating book, which quickens one with a

JOHN ADDINGTON SYMONDS

sense of the possibilities of life by its revelation of the charm, the courage, the nobility, the fixed aim, the endlessly thwarted and undaunted endeavour of a human spirit " to live resolvedly in the Whole, the Good, the Beautiful." To those who knew and loved the man, it calls up, not merely the blithe companion of any hour's adventure, but the real, suffering and sympathetic individuality that lay deeper ; and it recalls that memory with almost intolerable vividness.

In the early part of 1889 Symonds wrote an Autobiography, which he himself considered the best piece of literary work he had ever done. A good deal, especially of the earlier part, of this Autobiography is incorporated in Mr. Brown's volumes, and I am inclined to think that Symonds was right in his estimate of it. It is full of curious self-analysis of a nature which realizes itself to be "impenetrably reserved in the depths of myself, rhetorically candid on the surface." That, indeed, was Symonds' attitude through life ; and (strange, contradictory, as the man was in all things) even more so at the beginning than at the end of his career. Early in the Autobiography we find this curious description of a kind of trance which occurred at intervals up to the age ot twenty-eight.

Suddenly, at church or in company, or when I was reading, and always, I think, when my muscles were at rest, I felt the approach of the mood. Irresistibly it took possession of my mind and will, lasted what seemed an eternity, and disappeared in a series of rapid sensations, which resembled the awakening from anæsthetic influence. One reason why I disliked this kind of trance was that I could not describe it to myself. I cannot even now find words to render it intelligible, though it is probable that many readers of these pages will recognize the state in question. It consisted in a gradual but swiftly progressive obliteration of space, time, sensation, and the multitudinous factors of experience which seem to qualify what we are pleased to call ourself. In proportion as these conditions of ordinary consciousness were subtracted, the sense of an underlying or essential consciousness acquired intensity. At last nothing remained but a pure, absolute, abstract self. The universe became without form and void of content. But self persisted, formidable in its vivid keenness, feeling the most poignant doubt about reality, ready, as it seemed, to find existence break as breaks a bubble round about it. And what then ? The apprehension of a coming dissolution, the grim conviction that this state was the last state of the conscious self, the sense that I had followed the last thread of being to the verge of the abyss, and had arrived at demonstration of eternal Maya or illusion, stirred or seemed to stir me up again. The return to ordinary conditions of sentient existence began by my first recovering the power of touch, and then by the gradual though rapid influx of familiar impressions and diurnal interests. At last I felt myself once more a human being ; and though the riddle of what is meant by life remained unsolved, I was thankful for this return from the abyss—this deliverance from so awful an initiation into the mysteries of scepticism.

The record of this singular experience is but one of many revelations which we get in these pages of that brooding meditativeness which lay at the root of Symonds' nature ; that painfully minute introspection which finds more concrete expression in these passages from a Diary, written at the age of twenty-one :

I may rave, but I shall never rend the heavens: I may sit and sing, but I shall never make earth listen. And I am not strong enough to be good—what is left? I do not feel strong enough to be bad . . . The sum of intellectual progress I hoped for has been obtained, but how much below my hopes. My character has developed, but in what puny proportions, below my meanest anticipations. I do not feel a man. This book is an evidence of the yearnings without power, and the brooding self-analysis without creation that afflict me.

In all this there was a certain undoubted truth, and a part of the unhappiness of Symonds' life was certainly due to an only too precise sense of the limit of his own capacities, and an only too acute longing for an absolute achievement. "Women," he writes in a letter at the age of twenty-five, "do not, need not, pose themselves with problems about their own existence; but a man must do it, unless he has a fixed impulse in one definite direction, or an external force compelling him to take an inevitable line." Now, this was just what Symonds, even after the awakening of his ambition, even after the moment when Plato had in a sense revealed him to himself ("as though the voice of my own soul spoke to me through Plato") this was just what Symonds never had. We find him questioning himself:

If I give myself to literature, and find myself inadequate, can I be content with a fastidious silence? . . I feel so weak, so unable to do anything, or to take hold of any subject. In the room with me at this moment are five men, all provided with clear brains for business, all talking slang, and all wondering what strange incapable animal I am who have thus come among them.

And, again, in the Diary, we read:

> Why do I say "Lord, Lord," and do not? Here is my essential weakness. I wish and cannot will. I feel intensely, I perceive quickly, sympathize with all I see, or hear, or read. To emulate things nobler than myself is my desire. But I cannot get beyond—create, originate, win heaven by prayers and faith, have trust in God, and concentrate myself upon an end of action.

Here, indeed, we seem to be at the root of the great spiritual tragedy of his life, a tragedy of noble ambition, thwarted on every side, physically, morally, mentally. It was quite true that Symonds could create nothing, neither a well-balanced personality nor an achieved work of art. No one ever had a higher ideal of perfection, or strove more earnestly to reach it. But, as he well knew, there was something lacking, a certain disarray of faculties, and the full achievement never came. Those hesitations as to the path to pursue, law or literature, and, if literature, the special form of it, are significant. Every true artist is eternally doubtful of himself, eternally dissatisfied with the result of his best endeavours. But no true artist doubts in his heart of hearts whether the art of his choice is really the art for which he is best fitted. Himself he doubts, not his vocation. Now with Symonds the very impulse towards literature was a half-hearted one. He came to it as to a branch of culture; he toiled at it conscientiously, enthusiastically; but it was, in a certain sense, "work without hope," and it was also work done as a sort of gymnastic, a way of letting off energies. Much of Symonds' writing (most of it being so curiously impersonal, and yet not impersonal in the truly artistic way) was a means of escape, escape from himself. " Neither then nor afterwards," he writes, near the beginning of the Autobiography, " did I fear anything so much as my own self."

Symonds' detailed estimate of his own literary capacities and acquirements, in the Autobiography, is somewhat cruelly just:

Having an active brain and a lively curiosity, I was always acquiring information, while the defect of my retentive power made me continually lose the larger portion of it. Yet in this way my intellectual furniture grew to be a vague, ill-digested, inaccurate mass, rich in possibilities, but poor in solid stuff. . . . I cannot learn anything systematically. Grammar, logic, political economy, the exact sciences, offered insuperable difficulties to my mind. The result is, that I know nothing thoroughly, and I do not think this is so much due to laziness as to cerebral incapacity. . . . Retentive receptivity is the quality I claim. Combined with a moderate estimate of my own powers and a fair share of common sense, together with an active curiosity, this receptive and retentive susceptibility to various objects and emotions has given a certain breadth, a certain catholicity, a certain commonplaceness, to my æsthetic conclusions.

My powers of expression were considerable, yet not of first-rate quality. Vaughan, at Harrow, told me the truth when he said that my besetting sin was "fatal facility." I struggled long to conquer fluency. Still, I have not succeeded. I find a pleasure in expression for its own sake; but I have not the inevitable touch of the true poet, the unconquerable patience of the conscious artist. As in other matters, so here, I tried to make the best of my defects. Concentration lies beyond my grasp. The right words do not fall into the right places at my bidding. I have written few good paragraphs, and possibly no single perfect line.

Not a word need be added, nor a word altered, in this unsparing self-criticism. In truth, Symonds was neither a scholar nor an artist. What he possessed, however, was an extraordinarily interesting and unusual personality, which, gradually outgrowing the reserve and speculation of the earlier years, came at last to be intensely vivid, human, and acutely in touch with humanity. In 1877 he writes in a letter:

I, for my part, try to live without asking many questions. I do not want to be indifferent to the great problems of morals, immortality and the soul; but I want to learn to be as happy as my health and passions will allow me, without raising questions I am convinced no one will ever answer from our human standpoint.

It was a sort of awakening, this more human view of life; and, this sense of reality once firmly apprehended, he could write, as he does in one of his latest letters:

With me life burns ever more intense as my real strength wanes and my days decrease. It seems to me sometimes awful—the pace at which I live in feeling—inversely to the pace at which myself is ebbing to annihilation.

Gradually, therefore, a new estimate of the value, not merely of such literature as he could write, but of literature itself, formed itself in his mind; and united with that other feeling of powerlessness in still further discouraging him from too keen a following of art and the rewards of art. A passage which I may quote from an unpublished letter gives characteristic expression to this view of things:

> You are quite right to regard art, literature, as the noblest function of your life. What I gently said, and somewhat cynically, perhaps, to the contrary, is very much the result of a long experience in renunciation and patience, the like of which you have not yet had to undergo. I think it best for men to arm themselves with Stoicism as regards success (either external, or in proportion to their own ideals) and to maintain as a guiding principle what is the ultimate fact—namely, that art and literature are and never can be more than functions of human life. Life therefore first.

" Life therefore first." Symonds was right; and it was the life in him, the personality, that gave the man his real interest, his real fascination. But either he did not realize, or realized too late, that where he might have added something vital to literature was precisely in the record of this passionate communion with life. Perhaps, after all, "the right word" would never have "fallen into the right place." But, judging by the few personal things that he did, and by what we are allowed to read of that Autobiography, which is not likely at present to be published in its entirety, he might have done much; he would certainly have done something more essentially valuable than the never quite satisfying contributions to general culture, to which the main part of his life was devoted. But, as I have said, all this work was in part an escape, an escape from himself; and the "life" which he placed before "literature" was in part also an escape in another direction. Never "truly reconciled either with life or with himself," he chose the simpler task of writing the History of the Renaissance, rather than the perhaps impossible one of writing the history of his own soul.

IV NOTES AND IMPRESSIONS

II FRENCH WRITERS

THÉOPHILE GAUTIER

Théophile Gautier, like most Frenchmen who write at all, wrote enormously. He is exceptional, not in the quantity of his work, but in the quality. To be poet, novelist, and critic is nothing to a Frenchman; but it is not everyone who can write poetry like the *Emaux et Camées*, tales like the *Nouvelles*, and criticism like the *Portraits Contemporains;* to say nothing of such inspired Baedekers as the *Voyage en Espagne*. With Gautier the first need, the first capacity, was to write. The choice of subject was a quite secondary matter. He disliked the theatre, but, by a natural irony of fate, he spent a good deal of his life in writing dramatic criticisms, which, of course, he wrote admirably. Caring for quiet more than for most things, he was often obliged to write at the office of his paper, with an accompaniment obbligato of printing-presses. *Mademoiselle de Maupin* was written in six weeks, in the midst of every sort of distraction. For what lazy people call "inspiration" he had the contempt of a workmanlike man of letters. The Goncourts, in that brilliant early novel *Charles Demailly*, have put into the mouth of Masson, who stands for Gautier, a sort of confession of faith to which Gautier, in a whimsical moment, might well have given utterance. "I draw up my chair," says Masson to a *poseur* who has been setting forth his "system" of work; "I put on the table the paper, the pens, the ink, all the instruments of torture; and how it bores me! It has always bored me to write, and then it is so useless! Well, I write like that, deliberately, like a notary public. I do not go fast, but I am always going; for, you see, I don't search for the best. An article, a page, is like a child: either it is or it is not. I never think about what I am going to write. I take my pen and write. I am a man of letters: I ought to know my trade. Here is the paper before me; I am like the clown on his spring-board. And then I have a syntax very well in order in my head; I throw my phrases into the air—like cats! I am sure they will fall on their feet. It is quite simple: you only need to have a good syntax." So Gautier might really have said, knowing well just how much of sober truth went to the making of his paradoxes, which are not so paradoxical as they seem. What sounds like the confession of a contented hack is really the declaration of a perfectly accomplished master. For always, with Gautier, the work so hurriedly done, in seeming, was done with the same exquisite sense of form, the same exquisite finish of style. Apparently it was impossible for him to write badly. His style, like his handwriting, was so perfectly under his control, that it was equally out of the question for him to compose a badly-formed sentence or to pen a badly-formed letter. Never was a compliment more deserved than the title of " parfait magicien ès Lettres Françaises," under which Baudelaire dedicated the *Fleurs du Mal* to his " très-cher et très-vénéré maître et ami," Théophile Gautier.

Extreme attention to form is generally, and wrongly, supposed to indicate a certain disregard of substance, and the formula of " art for art's sake" has been taken to mean something very different from its real meaning. Gautier and Flaubert in France, Rossetti and Pater in England, are writers who have often been blamed by the critics for a carelessness about organic idea of which they are rarely enough guilty. It is not because a man's ideas are hazy that he takes care to give them rich and beautiful expression; but rather because his ideas are themselves precise and beautiful, and require to be expressed so that they may lose as little as possible in their translation into words. Gautier's mastery of form, as it happened, was natural and instinctive; unlike Flaubert, who agonized over the faultless composition of a sentence, he had only to take up his pen and write down the first words that presented themselves to his mind, certain that they would be the best words. Concise in his poetry, he is somewhat liberal of speech in his prose; where, also, he relies more on sonority; indulging, too, in what is conventionally called eloquence. But how faithful the style is everywhere to what it serves to express! an abounding wealth of contents, not exactly thought, it is true, but sensations and impressions, realized with an unparalleled freshness, directness, intensity. Gautier's outlook on life, and his view of his own work there, are expressed in that famous sentence, "I am a man for whom the visible world exists." M. Maxime du Camp, his biographer, contends that he literally invented descriptive prose; his descriptive verse is not less new in the explicit exactitude with which it reproduces things seen. Gautier, in prose and verse alike, is the poet of physical beauty, of the beauty of the exterior of things. *Mademoiselle de Maupin* that "golden book of spirit and sense," is one long ecstatic hymn to Beauty, the pagan, not the Christian, ideal: an ideal in which the soul counts for little or nothing, a grace of expression at most, and the lines and contours, the delights of form and colour, count for much. It is the same ideal, chastened, indeed, and less hotly followed, that we find in the carved and inlaid work of the *Emaux et Camées*. Gautier's poetry almost always resembles plastic art; and it is more often the art of the worker in marble or in onyx than the work of the painter. His prose is definitely pictorial: the outlines, always firm and precise if you search them out, are flooded with colour, bathed in atmosphere. Alike in poetry and in prose, what he gives us is, if we like to call it so, superficial: a man for whom the visible world existed, he was content with that world as his eyes saw it. But no, he was not content: this Greek in spirit, who remembered a former existence in which he walked with Pericles, had the same haunting sense of something strange and unknown, some distressing mystery in things, as the Greeks, the worshippers of beauty, who have left us a literature in which life is overshadowed by an inexorable Fatality. That singular and impressive poem, "La Comédie de la Mort," derives all its power from the shivering horror of its contemplation of death: exaggerated, *macabre*, one may call it; yet how natural a development of precisely that theory (habit, rather) of living by sensations! Just because he relishes the charm of life so keenly, because he cares so passionately for the human form, for the beauty of the visible world, Gautier dreads, more than most, the soiling and displacing touch of Death. So he has given expression, without intending it, to a whole philosophy, and seems to become the moralist of his own failure to be perfectly happy on the terms of the senses.

THÉODORE DE BANVILLE

"C'est certainement que cet homme a pour âme la Poésie elle-même," said an eloquent critic, not always so enthusiastic; and the word, in its pardonable exaggeration, is admirably descriptive. Banville, whether he wrote in verse or in prose, was a poet and nothing but a poet. Never was a man more absolutely devoted to, more entirely absorbed in, his art. He lived all his life in a state of poetic exaltation, not so much indifferent to external events as unconscious of them: I mean what are called important events, for he was Parisian of the Parisians, and delighted in the little incidents of the hour, which could be put into verse. But, though he loved nature and man, he loved art more than either; more than anything in the world, which was nevertheless so bright and satisfying to him. More than any poet of the day, he realized the joy of life, and with him, far more truly than with Gautier, of whom he says it,

> l'œuvre fut un hymne en fête
> A la vie ivre de soleil.

Among a great company of pessimistic poets, from Leconte de Lisle, with his calm and terrible

Nihilism, his troubled aspiration after the Nirvana of annihilation, to the petulaut and theatrical *Blasphèmes* of M. Richepin, Théodore de Banville remained true to the old faith (or should we call it the old heresy?) that the poet should be a messenger of joy, a singer of beauty. He had no theory of life to propound, except that spring is joyous, spring is fleeting, therefore gather the rosebuds while ye may:

> Aimer le vin,
> La beauté, le printemps divin,
> Cela suffit. Le reste est vain.

His philosophy is a frank, instinctive Epicureanism, a delighted acceptance of all that is delightful in the moments as they pass; with the least possible remembrance, if to remember is to regret, when they have gone for ever. It never occurred to him to question whether life was worth living, and he seems never to have supposed that this was not the best of all possible worlds. With so ingenuous a faith in things as they are, he laid himself open to the charge of being superficial; and, indeed, if it is the poet's duty to deal with what are called great questions, the questions that disturb the mind of the schoolmaster and the curate, then Banville failed in his duty. But if Ronsard, if Herrick, had any conception of the proper province of poetry, then Banville too, in his different, but not radically different way, was a poet.

Théodore de Banville was born at Moulins, March 14th, 1823. His father was a retired naval lieutenant, and it is to him that he dedicated his second book. His first book, *Les Cariatides*, published when he was nineteen, was dedicated to his mother, for whom, year by year, he made a little collection of birthday verses, finally published, in 1878, under the name of *Roses de Noël*. Banville's life was uneventful: it has a date to mark his birth, a date (sixty-eight years later, almost to a day) to mark his death. He never married, he was not elected to the Academy, he had no special and startling triumphs in a literary career which was long, honoured, and successful. "A poet whose life has been modest and unobserved," he said, "has no biography but his works." *Les Cariatides*, his first volume, was a remarkable achievement for a poet of nineteen. The influence of Hugo, whom Banville never ceased to worship as the poet of poets, was naturally evident. The whole book is quite in the early romantic manner, with stanzas full of proper names, poems addressed to the Venus of Milo, poems about sultanas. But there is also, already, the soaring lyric flight, and even a certain power of sustaining the flight. The boy has a vocabulary, and if he has not yet a style, he knows very well, at all events, how to say what he wants to say. And there are *dixains* in the manner of Clément Marot, rondeaux, rondeaux rédoublés, triolets; experiments in those old forms that Banville has done so much to bring into use again. *Les Stalactites*, as the author tells us, from the standpoint of twenty-three, are decidedly more mature than *Les Cariatides*. That fundamental characteristic of Banville, lyric joy, had indeed been evident from the first, but here it breaks forth more spontaneously, more effectually. " An immense appetite for happiness and hope lies at the root of our souls. To reconquer the lost joy, to remount with intrepid foot the azure stairway leading to the skies " : such, Banville tells us in his preface, is the incessant aspiration of modern man ; his own aspiration, he should have said. In 1852 appeared a characteristic little play, *Le Feuilleton d'Aristophane*, the best, perhaps, as it is the most famous, of Banville's lyric dramas. It is a sort of *revue de l'année*, done with immense spirit and gaiety, and with a wealth of real poetry instead of the usual meagre measure of doggrel. It is full of wit and of a fantastic, essentially modern kind of poetry, which is yet entirely individual. The play was followed by some charming books of prose (*Les Pauvres Saltimbanques, La Vie d'une Comédienne*) and then came a little volume of *Odelettes* (1856) a book of spring verses, dedicated by Banville to his friends. Next year appeared anonymously, in a quaintly got-up green-covered pamphlet, the *Odes Funambulesques*.

" The ' Odes Funambulesques ' have not been signed," said the preface, " because they were not worth the trouble." " Here are fantasies assuredly more than frivolous; they will do nothing to change the constitution of society, and they have not even, like some poems of our time, the excuse of genius. Worse, the ideal boundary which marks the limits of good taste is overstepped at every moment, and, as M. Ponsard judiciously remarks, in a line which should survive his works, if the works themselves do not remain immortal:

> When that is overstepped, there is no limit left!"

So the author introduces his rope-dancing verses. Their allusiveness renders some of them difficult for the readers of to-day, yet they have the qualities that remain. To be familiar, to be jocular, to burlesque the respectabilities, to overflow into parody, to exhibit every kind of rhythmical agility; to dance on the tight-rope of verse, and yet to be always poetical, always the lyric poet, is a feat which few have ever accomplished, a feat which Banville has never accomplished so deftly as in these wittily-named *Odes Funambulesques*. There is a series of *Occidentales*, parodies of Hugo's *Orientales*; there are satires in the stately manner, and satires which explode into sparks like fireworks; there are rondeaux, triolets, pantoums. Juvenal-Pierrot, Boileau-Harlequin, as Barbey d'Aurevilly called him, Banville has spread a feast of light-hearted gaiety which has even now a certain savour. Here is an untranslatable triolet, the whole fun of which depends on the rhymes; preposterously clever rhymes which sing themselves over in one's head through a whole evening:

> Mademoiselle Michonnet
> Est une actrice folichonne.
> Autrefois chacun bichonnait
> Mademoiselle Michonnet.
> Le public qui la bouchonnait
> Dans ses dents aujourd'hui mâchonne:
> Mademoiselle Michonnet
> Est une actrice folichonne.

In the same year with the *Odes Funambulesques*, a collection of some of Banville's most serious and "heightened" work was printed under the name of *Le Sang de la Coupe*, and in 1866 (after more plays and more books of prose) appeared his finest volume of serious poems, *Les Exilés*, and his finest play, *Gringoire*, well known to English playgoers under the name of *The Ballad-Monger*.

In the preface to *Les Exilés* Banville writes: "This book is perhaps the one into which I have put the most of myself and my soul, and if one book of mine is to last, I would desire that it should be this one." This book, into which he tells us he has put the most of himself, is entirely impersonal, and it is characteristic of Banville that this should be so. What was deepest in him was a passion for art, for poetry, which to him was literally, and not figuratively, something inspired. "Like the art of antiquity, his art," said Gautier, "expresses only what is beautiful, joyous, noble, grand, rhythmical." The poems in *Les Exilés* are mainly on classical subjects; they have always a measure of classic charm, a large, clear outline, a purity of line, a suave colour. There is fire in them as well as grace; some of them are painted with hot flesh-tints, as "Une Femme de Rubens." But the classical note predominates, and in such verse as this, written for "La Source" of Ingres, there is none of the romantic trouble, but a clear silver flow, the sweep of broad and placid rhythms:

> Oh! ne la troublez pas! La solitude seule
> Et le silence ami par son souffle adouci
> Ont le droit de savoir pourquoi sourit ainsi
> Blanche, oh! si blanche, avec ses rougeurs d'églantine,
> Debout contre le roc, la Naïade argentine!

In the *Idylles Prussiennes* published in 1872, Banville returned to the composition of "occasional poems," this time ironical and indignant, and touched with the tragedy of daily events: they were printed Monday by Monday in *Le National* during the siege of Paris. Then, in 1874, he published a charming series of sonnets, *Les Princesses*, on "those great Princesses whose mysterious eyes, whose red lips, have been, through all the ages, the desire and delight of all humankind." More books of prose followed, *Contes*, *Souvenirs*, *Esquisses Parisiennes* with a *Petit Traité de Poésie Française*, the most poetically written of all textbooks to poetry, the most dogmatic, by no means the least practical, and altogether the most inspiring. The volume called *Mes Souvenirs*, sketches and anecdotes of most of the Romantics, known and unknown, is the most charming book of literary *souvenirs* in the world. In 1884 came another volume of effervescent verse, *Nous Tous;* and in 1890 a new collection, *Sonnailles et Clochettes*, poems published in newspapers, really journalistic verse, which is really poetry. It is a new art, which it amused Banville to invent and practise; for how amusing it is, he said, "to offer people pebbles of Eldorado, pearls and diamonds, saying gaily: Only a penny a-piece!"

Banville's poetry astonishes one, first of all, by its virtuosity. He is the greatest master of rhyme who has ever used the French language, a perfect Ingoldsby; one of the greatest masters of rhythm and poetical technique, a very Swinburne. But he is not merely great by reason of his form. It is true that he has no passion and little that can be called intellectual substance. His verse is nothing but verse, but it is that; it is sheer poetry, with no other excuse for its existence than this very sufficing reason, its own beauty. Banville sometimes deals with splendid subjects, as in the "Malédiction de Cypris," but he never sought very carefully for subjects; confident of his singing-voice, he sang. And he sang of the eternal commonplaces, eternally poetical; of the nightingale, the night and the stars, of April and the flowers, of wine and of song, of loves as light and charming as their classic names. He could write:

> Ruisseaux! forêts! silence!
> O mes amours d'enfance!

and yet turn these trite old "properties" into poetry. What he wrote was mostly "occasional verse," but with him "occasional verse" was transformed into abiding poetry. That has been done before, by Herrick, for example, but whenever it is done it is an achievement, and Banville, alone among modern poets, has won this difficult success.

HENRY MURGER

Paris has its bust of Murger now, the Latin Quarter had its brave day's enthusiasm, and the academic criticism, and the criticism of the pitiless *jeunes*, have wearied a little of repeating the old arguments against Bohemia, against the *Scènes de la Vie de Bohême*. Murger has his faults as a writer: it cannot be said that his prose is distinguished, his taste impeccable, his tears or his laughter quite invariably convincing. But he has written a book that lives, and there is no arguing against such a fact. It has been gravely enquired whether these *Scènes de la Vie de Bohême* are true to life; whether Musette, Rodolphe, and Mimi are probable characters; whether the sentiment of the whole thing is not false sentiment. People ask strange questions! As long as men and women are young, and not quite virtuous, so long will this kind of life exist, just thus; and never has it been rendered so simply, sympathetically, and with so youthful a touch of sentiment, as in Murger's pages. And this sentiment, is it false sentiment? It is the sentiment youth has of itself at the flowering moment of existence; and to whom, and in what sense, does a disillusioning experience give the right to deny the "truth" of a sentiment which had at least the irresistible force of a sensation? To be five-and-twenty, poor, and in love: that is enough; at that age, and under those circumstances, you will feel that Murger has said everything. They tell us that the Latin Quarter has changed, that the *grisette* no longer exists, that people are quite cynical and serious now-a-days, and that

la belle
Qui m'aima quand elle eut le temps

has no time now. Ah! there is always time for these little distractions, when one cares to indulge in them; and youth, after all, is not so variable a quantity as our historians would have us imagine. Fashions change, the curls and the crinolines; but not "the way of a man with a maid." And that is what Murger has fixed for us in these impromptu-like pages, not in the fine impersonal way of the outside observer, but gaily, pathetically, as such moods make up the joy and pity of our ways of loving.

Full of fun as the book is, of keen wit and exuberant humour, it is one of the saddest of books, sad with the consciousness that

La jeunesse n'a qu'un temps.

All these merry, shifting, shiftless people seem continually to be saying "Let us eat and drink, for to-morrow we die;" they have the feverish gaiety of the gambler who has staked all on one throw. It is all for love; and love, with them, is known as much by its bitter inconstancy as by its momentary sweetness. "Muse de l'infidélité," Murger addresses the eternal Musette, in that song which is part of her immortality:

> Non, ma jeunesse n'est pas morte,
> Il n'est pas mort ton souvenir;
> Et si tu frappais à ma porte,
> Mon cœur, Musette, irait t'ouvrir.
> Puisqu'à ton nom toujours il tremble,
> Muse de l'infidélité,
> Reviens encor manger ensemble
> Le pain béni de la gaité.

Love, with him, as Gautier pointed out, "presents itself only as a memory." It is at least always apprehended, even at the sharpest moment of enjoyment, as but the flash of the foam on the crest of a wave breaking.

And then, along with this pathetic feeling in regard to love, there is another, more sordid, not less actual, kind of pathos: the cold of winter nights in a garret, the odour of rich men's dinners as one passes penniless in the street. These people are very genuinely poor, and they discover no hidden treasures. They want, too, to be famous, and they have neither the talent nor the luck for even that, the poor man's consolation. They see the hospital at the end of the way; at most they divine it around the corner. And meanwhile there is the reality of day by day, the necessity of a few poor luxuries: Mimi's bonnet, Francine's muff. Here, once more, is a sentiment which only the quite rich and fortunate can distinguish as "false."

Yes, Murger is a veracious historian; believe him, if you do not know, or have forgotten, that such are the annals of Bohemia. There, people love just so lightly and sincerely, weep and laugh just so freely, are really hungry, really have their ambitions, and at times die of all these maladies. It is the gayest and most melancholy country in the world. Not to have visited it, is to have made the grand tour for nothing. To have lived there too long, is to find all the rest of the world an exile. But if you have been there or not, read Murger's pages; there, perhaps, after all, you will see more of the country than anything less than a lifetime spent in it will show you.

BENJAMIN CONSTANT

THE *Journal Intime* of Benjamin Constant, only lately published in its entirety, is one of the most curious and instructive human documents that have been provided for the surprise and enlightenment of the student of souls. "Une des singularités de ma vie," wrote the author of *Adolphe*, in a letter to a friend, "c'est d'avoir toujours passé pour l'homme le plus insensible et le plus sec et d'avoir été constamment gouverné et tourmenté par des sentiments indépendants de tout calcul et même destructifs de tous mes intérêts de position, de gloire et de fortune." And, indeed, there was not a single interest, out of the many that occupied his life, which he did not destroy by some inconsequence of action, for no reason in the world, apparently, except some irrational necessity of doing exactly the opposite of what he ought to have done, of what he wanted to do. "Si je savais ce que je veux, je saurais mieux ce que je fais," he wrote once; and through all his disturbed and inexplicable existence, he was never able to make up his mind, at least for a sufficient period, as to what he really wanted. Love, political power, and literary fame were the three main interests of his life; and it was the caprice of his nature, in regard to all three, to build with one hand while he pulled down his own work with the other. How well he knew his own weakness this Journal shows us on every page. "Heureux," he writes, "qui se replie sur lui-même, qui ne demande point de bonheur, qui vit avec sa pensée et attend la mort sans s'épuiser en vaines tentatives pour adoucir ou embellir sa vie!" He seems always, somewhat unreasonably, to have held out such an ideal before himself, and it was one of his dissatisfactions never to have attained it. He tells us somewhere: "La meilleure qualité que le ciel m'ait donnée, *c'est celle de m'amuser de moi-même*." But this was precisely what he could never do, in any satisfying measure; at best it was a very bitter kind of amusement. He fled himself, to find refuge, if he might, among others; like his own Adolphe, who tells us, in a memorable sentence, "je me reposais, pour ainsi dire, dans l'indifférence des autres, de la fatigue de son amour." But the indifference of others drove him back upon himself; and so, all through life, he found himself tossed to and fro, always irresolute, always feverishly resolved to take some decided step, and, at times, taking it, always at the disastrous moment. "Il faut se décider, agir et se taire," he writes in his Journal, fully conscious that he will never do any of the three. And he laments: "Si dans six mois je ne suis pas hors de tous ces embarras qui, en réalité, n'existent que dans ma tête, je ne suis qu'un imbécile et je ne me donnerai plus la peine de m'écouter."

He was never tired of listening to himself, and the acute interest of this Journal consists in the absolute sincereity of its confessions, and at the same time the scrutinizing self-consciousness of every word that is written down. "Il y a en moi deux personnes," as he truly says, "dont l'une observe l'autre"; and he adds: "Ainsi, dans ce moment, je suis triste, mais si je voulais, je serais, non pas consolé, mais tellement distrait de ma peine qu'elle serait comme nulle." Thus when one who was perhaps his best friend, Mlle. Talma, was dying, he spends day and night by her bedside, overwhelmed with grief; and he writes in his Journal: "J'y étudie la mort." His own conclusion from what he has observed in himself is: "Je ne suis pas tout à fait un être réel." On the contrary, he is very real, with that distressing kind of reality which afflicts the artist, and out of which, after he has duly suffered for it, he creates his art, as Benjamin Constant created *Adolphe*. *Adolphe*, a masterpiece of psychological narrative, from which the modern novel of analysis may be said to have arisen, is simply a human document, in which Benjamin Constant has told the story of his *liaison* with Madame de Staël. Look at the Journal, and you will see how abundantly the man suffered. "Tous les volcans sont moins flamboyants qu'elle"; "rupture décisive": this on one page, and on the next, "Madame de Staël m'a reconquis." A few pages further on: "Je sens que je passerais pour un monstre si je la quitte; je mourrai si je ne la quitte pas. Je la regrette et je la hais." And the next line tells us that he has returned to her side, "malheureux que je suis!" He suffers because he can neither be entirely absorbed, nor, for one moment, indifferent; that very spirit of analysis, which would seem to throw some doubt on the sincerity of his passion, does but intensify the acuteness with which he feels it. It is like the turning of the sword in a wound. Coldness it certainly is not, though it produces the effect of coldness; selfishness it may be, but is anything more sincere, or more certain to produce its own misery, than just that quality of selfishness common to all exacting lovers? No, Benjamin Constant, as this Journal shows him to us, was a very real being; singularly human in his inconsequences, the fever and exhaustion of his desires, the impossible gifts he asked of Fate, the impossible demands he made upon himself and others. He sums up and typifies the artistic temperament at its acutest point of weakness; the temperament which can neither resist, nor dominate, nor even wholly succumb to, emotion; which is for ever seeking its own hurt, with the persistence almost of mania; which, if it ruins other lives in the pursuit, as is supposed, of artistic purposes, gains at all events no personal satisfaction out of the bargain; except, indeed, when one has written *Adolphe*, the satisfaction of having lived unhappily for more than sixty years, and left behind one a hundred pages that are still read with admiration, sixty years afterwards.

GUY DE MAUPASSANT

As a writer, Maupassant was "de race," as the French say; he was the lineal descendant of the early *conteurs*. Trained under the severe eye of the impeccable Flaubert, he owed infinitely, no doubt, to that training, and much to the actual influence of the great novelist, who, in *L'Éducation Sentimentale*, has given us the type of the modern novel. But his style is quite different from that of Flaubert, of which it has none of the splendid, subdued richness, the harmonious movement; it is clear, precise, sharply cut, without ornament or elaboration; with much art, certainly, in its deliberate plainness, and with the admirable skill of an art which conceals art. M. Halévy has aptly applied to him the saying of Vauvenargues: "La netteté est le vernis des maîtres." Not Swift himself had a surer eye or hand for the exact, brief, malicious notation of things and ideas. He seems to use the first words that come to hand, in the order in which they naturally fall; and when he has reached this point he stops, not conceiving that there is anything more to be done. So, if he has not invented a new style, like Goncourt, he has carried on the tradition of French prose, faultlessly.

As a novelist, Maupassant has done remarkable and admirable work; but it is as a *conteur* that he is supreme, and it is in his *contes* that he will live. As a writer of the *nouvelle*, or short story, Maupassant has no rival. He saw exactly so much of nature in general, and exactly so much of a given incident or emotion, as could be realized within the limits of a short story, in which there would be just room for a clear, firm statement of the facts. His ability in selecting and fitting his material, threatened to become mechanical, a skill of the hand merely; but it never did so. Compare one of his tales with a tale of even so brilliant a story-writer as Mr. Kipling, and his supremacy in this difficult art manifests itself at once. A tale by Mr. Kipling is merely an anecdote; an anecdote of the most vivid kind, but nothing more. What is lacking? Just that which seems to count for so little, and which really counts for so much: the moral idea. With Maupassant, the moral idea is always there, at the root of what may seem at first a mere anecdote; it is there, permeating the whole substance of the story, giving it its vitality, and its place in the organism of nature. Every story is thus rounded, and becomes complete in itself by becoming the part of a great whole. Even

Maupassant's cynicism, which was fundamental, and which sent him for his subjects to the seamy side, always, of things, could not vitiate in him this principle of all great art. His apprehension of what I call the moral idea was certainly not what in England is called moral; and it must be admitted that much of his work is unnecessarily, wantonly unpleasant, and that most of it is not quite needfully sordid. But, being professedly not a psychologist, being content to leave the soul out of the question, he found that the animal passions were at the root of our nature, that they gave rise to the most vivid and interesting kinds of action, and he persisted in rendering mainly the animal side of life. Probably no writer has ever done so more convincingly, with a more thorough knowledge of his subject, and a more perfect mastery of his knowledge. In his later work he seemed to be trying his hand at psychology, to be beginning to concern himself about the soul. It was a deviation from his true path, the path of his success; and the avenging madness came to save him, as he is now finally saved by death, from the fatality of a possible "ascent" out of his solid and sufficing materialism.

LECONTE DE LISLE

THE death of Leconte de Lisle deprived France of one of the most remarkable poets of the present age. The successor in the Academy to the chair of Victor Hugo, he had been to a certain degree the successor of Victor Hugo in a sort of leadership in poetry. Perhaps the first definite signs of the wane of Hugo's influence might be traced in the Parnassian movement, of which Leconte de Lisle was the acknowledged head. That movement having had its day, and a new school taken its place, Leconte de Lisle has long since lost all influence as an active force. It is the fashion, indeed, in Paris just now, among the younger men, to deny that he was a poet at all. Such monstrous injustice is equally unjust to the catholic-minded poet in whose honour this last dethronement has been made; for has not Paul Verlaine written, "Leconte de Lisle est un grand et noble poète"?

Charles Marie René Leconte de Lisle was born in the island of Réunion, October 23rd, 1818. His first volume, the *Poèmes Antiques*, was published in 1853; *Poèmes et Poésies* followed in 1855; then came *Poèmes Barbares*; *Poèmes Tragiques*; *Les Erinnyes* and *L'Apollonide*, two classical dramas, both of which have been acted at the Odéon; and he has translated into prose, with extraordinarily sympathetic literalness, Homer, Hesiod, Theocritus, Æschylus, Sophocles, Euripides, Virgil, and Horace. Never was a poet more actually and more fundamentally a scholar; and his poetry both gains and loses, but certainly becomes what it is, through this scholarship, which was not merely concerned with Greece and Rome, but with the East as well; a scholarship not only of texts, but of the very spirit of antiquity. That tragic calmness which was his favourite attitude towards life and fate; that haughty dissatisfaction with the ugliness and triviality of the present, the pettiness and unreason of humanity; that exclusive worship of immortal beauty; that single longing after the annihilating repose of Nirvana; was it not the all-embracing pessimism (if we like to call it, for convenience, by such a name) which is the wisdom of the East, modified, certainly, by a temperament which had none of the true Eastern serenity? In spite of his theory of impassibility, Leconte de Lisle has expressed only himself, whether through the mouth of Cain or of Hypatia; and in the man, as I just knew him, I seemed to see all the qualities of his work; in the rigid, impressive head, the tenacity of the cold eyes, the ideality of the forehead, the singularly unsensuous lips, a certain primness, even, in the severity, the sarcasm, of the mouth. Passion in Leconte de Lisle is only an intellectual passion;

emotion is never less than epical; the self which he expresses through so many immobile masks is almost never a realizable human being, who has lived and loved. Thus it is, not merely that all this splendid writing, so fine as literature in the abstract, can never touch the multitude, but that for the critic of literature also there is a sense of something lacking. Never was fine work in verse so absolutely the negation of Milton's three requirements, that poetry should be simple, sensuous, and passionate. And, perhaps, in spite of the remarkable originality of "Les Eléphants," "Les Hurleurs," and all that group of exotic flora and fauna; in spite of the tragic irony of "Un Acte de Charité" and its companion pieces; in spite of all the scholarly and all the curious work which he did in so many kinds, the most really poetic part of his poetry, that by which he will live, is to be found in such poems as "Requies" and "Le Dernier Souvenir," in which he has said, with perfect simplicity and with perfect calmness, all there is to be said of the actual emptiness of life, and the possible horror of death.

M. CATULLE MENDÈS

M. CATULLE MENDÈS has the curious, and scarcely enviable, distinction of having done nearly everything, in literature, nearly as well as everybody. His earlier verse, in the manner of Hugo, is hardly to be distinguished from genuine Hugo; his Parnassian verse is so pre-eminently Parnassian that it may almost be taken as the type of that manner; when he tired of doing impeccable Leconte de Lisle, he did faultless Banville and almost deceptive Verlaine. And, indeed, he may be said to have invented some of his masters, whom (M. François Coppée for instance) he certainly started on the road of letters. In prose he has written novels which partake of the *roman à clef*, the *succès de scandale*, and the *document humain*, novels which are at all events written in beautiful French, a little subtle and perverse, but full of surprising and delicious graces. And he has done the most elegantly improper short stories that can be conceived, fairy tales of such ethereal innocence that they might be read by little winged angels; he has invented adorable ballets, written librettos more musical than the music to which they were set; and he has given to all the worthier of his contemporaries the most just and ungrudging praise of any contemporary critic. Then he is one of the best talkers in Paris; at fifty he looks like his own younger brother; in life and in literature, he is one of the successes of the day. And, in its way, his success is deserved; for, in his way, he is a true man of letters. His misfortune is to be a man of letters who has nothing to say, or in other words, who can say everthing. With equal indifference, with equal ease, he addresses

> Cypris, fille de l'onde, adorable chimère,.
> Immortelle aux yeux noirs, Reine au cœur indulgent,
> Qui mires la beauté dans les hymnes de Homère!

and, in laughing stanzas, Peppa Invernizzi of the Opera:

> Mousse aux galères de Watteau,
> Fine lèvre, œil mi-clos qui cligne,
> Tu fus le Gille, aile maligne,
> Posé sur un pizzicato;

and both are alike to him "but as the sound of lyres and flutes." What is amazing is that even in his most frivolous verse (in the latest volume for instance, *La Grive des Vignes*) he never, even when he must be in reality most sincere, gets a convincing sincerity in expression. Verse which is really the exact utterance of no matter how fleeting, how trivial, how unworthy, a moment of real sincerity, assures its own immortality. When Rochester writes:

> Give me leave to rail at you,
> I ask nothing but my due;
> To call you false, and then to say
> You shall not keep my heart a day:
> But, alas! against my will,
> I must be your captive still.
> Ah! be kinder then; for I
> Cannot change, and would not die;

he expresses, with only the natural sophistication of the lover, a truly human sentiment. But the fatal fact is that M. Catulle Mendès expresses, not the human but the Parisian sentiment; and so we get, even when there is really some personal feeling at the back of it, *l'article de Paris*, and no more. No problem in literature is more curious than the question of what constitutes poetic sincerity, and how that quality is attained. It is apparently independent of poetic craftsmanship, or certainly M. Mendès could have compassed it, and yet it can rarely be achieved without a consummate and conscious art, or how many minor poets (who really mean well) would have achieved it! With M. Mendès, however, there is a defect in the intention: he does not write because something calls for expression, but because he would like to express something prettily. His devotion to form is unbounded, but he does not realize that form depends on ideas, and that the most ingenious words in the world cannot make ideas. In his prose, these defects of his qualities are somewhat less conspicuous, somewhat less irretrievable, because his prose is mostly fiction, and fiction must at least have so much of fact in it as to deal with human life and the actualities of society. So it is that the best work he has ever done is to be found in a novel called *La Femme Enfant* in which his gracious, flimsy, and perverse talent has for once found a subject as gracious, flimsy, and perverse as itself. Liliane, the depraved little ballet-girl, whose virginal innocence of face is but the flower of a soul in which vice has sprung, unconscious of itself, is a type which has never been so perfectly expressed before, a type whose very artificiality, is, for once, truly human. Here, to my mind, M. Mendès has achieved his one really serious success, and it is because he has had something to say, because the idea has made the book. Yet he remains, for the warning of all clever people, the cleverest of them all, clever to the point of self-annihilation; and his work, charming, elegant, accomplished, with all the semblance of what it is not, the work too of a man of letters, but of a man of letters who writes to please, pleases, certainly, for its moment; and then, the moment after, has melted away, like the snows of yesterday, or yesterday's ice at Jullien's.

M. ANATOLE FRANCE

M. Anatole France is a man of letters, *amateur* in the fine sense, who would willingly have you believe him something of the amateur in the looser and more current meaning of the word. He has attempted a good many things, somewhat different in kind from one another, in which he has shown an extreme care and scrupulousness in the matter of writing, a sincere endeavour after no limited or facile sort of perfection, and, especially, a fixed determination that literature, with him, shall be literature. He has written criticism, fiction, and verse. It is probable that he is a slow worker, and that his work costs him a considerable labour. But it amuses him to seem aloof from his work, a little careless, a little disdainful of it, even, and to admit: "J'en parle avec un absolu désinteressement, étant, par nature, fort détaché des choses, et disposé à me demander chaque soir, avec l'Ecclésiaste: 'Quel fruit revient à l'homme de tout l'ouvrage?'" He looks back with regret to the time when he was a student, not a writer. "J'ai vécu d'heureuses années sans écrire. Je menais une vie contemplative et solitaire dont le souvenir m'est encore infiniment doux." In the preface to the first volume of *La Vie Littéraire*, he explains how the editor of *Le Temps* drew him out of his seclusion, and forced him to become a critic, a service for which every one must be profoundly grateful to M. Hébrard. For it is as a critic that he has, perhaps, the largest claim on our attention, a critic of so personal a kind that he is at the same time an artist, even when he writes of the latest *nouvelle* of Gyp.

Criticism, M. France tells us on one page, "flottera toujours dans l'incertitude. Ses lois ne seront point fixes, ses jugements ne seront point irrévocables. Bien différente de la justice, elle fera peu de mal et peu de bien, si toutefois c'est faire peu de bien que d'amuser un moment les âmes délicates et curieuses." Do not credit the caprice of so characteristic a modesty; that is not what he believes at all. Turn rather to another page, and read there: "Je crois que la critique, ou plutôt l'essai littéraire, est une forme exquise de l'histoire. Je dis plus: elle est la vraie histoire, celle de l'esprit humain. Elle exige, pour être bien traitée, des facultés rares et une culture savante. Elle suppose un affinement intellectuel que de longs siècles d'art ont pu seuls produire. C'est pourquoi elle ne se montre que dans les sociétés déjà vieilles, à l'heure exquise des premiers declins." And, to add a sentence from yet another page: "La critique est la dernière en date de toutes les formes littéraires; elle finira peut-être par les absorber toutes." But what is it that M. France understands by criticism? "Mon affaire," he assures us, "n'est point d'analyser les livres: j'ai assez fait quand j'ai suggéré quelque haute curiosité au lecteur bienveillant." Or, in his famous definition: "Le bon critique est celui qui raconte les aventures de son âme au milieu des chefs-d'œuvre." It is an exquisite definition, exquisitely true of M. France himself. It would be easy to say that he is not a critic at all. But then he only professes to give us something of himself, as that something reveals itself at the contact of other minds, other souls, preserved to us in books. A book, for him, is "une œuvre de sorcellerie d'où s'échappent toutes sortes d'images qui troublent les espirits et changent les cœurs." It delights him to come under this magic influence, he surrenders himself to it with a smiling, confident, sceptical, and adventurous curiosity. He loves a book as a man might love a woman, and his criticism is a sort of fine flattery, or discreet raillery, full of sensibility, of intellectual emotion, in which a profound and exact learning disguises itself in order to be charming. What he says of Hamlet may be said of himself: "Il pense tour à tour comme un moine du moyen âge et comme un savant de la Renaissance; il a la tête philosophique et pourtant pleine de diableries." He is a survival of the Humanists of the Renaissance, with his intellectual curiosity in life and legend, in moral problems and the actual vices of real or imaginary people, in his urbane, philosophic malice, his gentle and pitiless wit. Naturally tolerant, sympathetic, benign, and at the same time " sûr de très peu de choses en ce monde," he is very certain of stupidity or pretence when he sees it, and if, despite his aversion, he is obliged to contemplate and to comment upon it, his irony, in its very gentleness, has the cruelty of a cat holding a mouse between its velvet paws. Read him, for example, on M. Georges Ohnet. But that amusing castigation is scarcely typical of a writer who, like his master in so many things, Renan, prefers a certain elegance in evasion. He is always, in his own fashion, sincere; but he would rather not always be quite definite. " Sure of so little in this world," it pleases him to leave most large questions open; to discriminate without prejudice, to praise without rivalry, to dissent with an amiable smile : " No doubt there is quite as much, or nearly, to be said for your way of thinking as for mine ! "

Creative, to a certain extent, in his criticism, the artist of a series of exquisite " confessions," M. France is always something of a critic in his fiction. There is just so much truth in that pose of his as an amateur in letters, that all his works are somewhat deliberate excursions in one direction or another, experiments, sometimes, one fancies, done in order to show that they can be done, not from any very urgent impulse from within. As he is both a man of letters and a scholar, it is natural that he should have been tempted by legendary and mediæval subjects; and in *Thais*, for example, we have an admirable piece of craftsmanship, done absolutely from without, very beautifully and sympathetically, but with an art in which there is at all events no moment of illusion: sentiment, costume, *décor*, emotion, all are rendered with a sort of conscious propriety. The feeling, troubling as that would be if it were realized acutely, never touches us with any real sense of pity; it is treated with too elegant an aloofness, almost decoratively, as a remote, curious thing. It is antiquity apprehended, not as real life, really lived once long ago, but as ancient history, as recorded legend. In one book, however, *Le Lys Rouge*, which is a novel of contemporary life, he has succeeded in realizing and in making us realize that quality of direct emotion which never elsewhere fully expresses itself in the rest of his elegant and exquisite work. It is a study in "modern love," the passion, with its curiosities of sentiment and sensation, its ecstasies and cruelties, set in a framework of literary and artistic society, some of the persons in which are exact portraits of real persons, Paul Verlaine, for instance. Here, for once, the scholar passes almost wholly into the sensitive, sympathetic artist; the gentle Epicurean, who smiles so urbanely upon the great and little distractions by which humanity amuses itself in that short interval given to it, is content to be absorbed in one or two definite men and women, to whom these distractions (as seen by the philosophic eye) are the only serious things in life. " La vérité," as he tells us in a later, more reflective book, *Le Jardin d'Epicure*, " la vérité est que la vie est délicieuse, horrible, charmante, affreuse, douce, amère, et qu'elle est tout." And *Le Lys Rouge* gives us the sense of what is delicious, and horrible, and charming, and atrocious, and sweet, and bitter, in life lived fatally, absorbingly, exceptionally, as to the circumstances, and the course of them, in those passions by which alone we truly live. The scholar's subtlety has turned inwards upon the heart, and here, in this beautiful, painful, fascinating book, which really hurts one, we find what we have never found before in a writer who has been only too exclusively a literary man. " Et tout le reste est littérature!" we have now the excuse of saying, in that only comparatively disdainful outburst of Verlaine; and it is, after all, not as the writer of *Le Lys Rouge* that M. France presents himself under his normal aspect. Let us not try to sum him up, to bring him under any formula, to explain why he is what he is, and why he has his exceptions from himself; let us leave him a little vague, infinitely charming, not quite satisfying if he is to be judged among the great writers; an artist in style, in thought, in sensibility, in scholarship; not a critic, as the world looks upon criticism, yet above all, in the fine sense, a critic, of literature and of life; definitely at least, and finally, a man of letters, the typical scholar of letters of our day.

M. HUYSMANS AS A MYSTIC

To the student of psychology, few more interesting cases could be presented than the development of M. Huysmans. He began his literary career, nearly twenty years ago, as a realist, more unflinchingly absorbed in the ugliness of reality than even Zola himself. *Marthe: Historie d'une Fille*, published at Brussels in 1876, is one of the most brutal books ever written. *Les Sœurs Vatard* and *En Ménage*, which followed, are both sordid studies in the most sordid side of life; it is with all the dull persistence of hate that they detail, gloatingly, the long and dreary chronicle of insignificant, disagreeable, daily distresses. The end of *En Ménage* leaves us with this note of despairing resignation: " Peut-être bien que l'éternelle bêtise de l'humanitié voudra de nous, et que, semblable à nos concitoyens, nous aurons ainsi qu'eux le droit de vivre enfin respectés et stupides ! " In *A Rebours* the realist has outgrown the creeds and the methods of realism, and we have an astonishing picture of the artificial paradise in which a perverse imagination can isolate itself in the midst of all the healthy and intolerable commonplaces of contemporary existence. The book is the one real, the one quintessential, book which has been produced by the literature vaguely called decadent. And, in giving final expression to this theory of the charm of what is diseased, unnaturally beautiful, to this lust of strange sensations, it ends with an even more hopeless cry of dissatisfaction: " Seigneur, prenez pitié du chrétien qui doute, de l'incrédule qui voudrait croire, du forçat de la vie qui s'embarque seul, dans la nuit, sous un firmament qui n'éclairent plus les consolants fanaux du vieil espoir!" In *Là-Bas* we are in yet another stage of this strange pilgrim's progress. The disgust which once manifested itself in the merely external revolt against the ugliness of streets, the stupidity of faces, has become more and more internalized, and the attraction of what is perverse in the unusual beauty of art has led, by some obscure route, to the perilous half-way house of a corrupt mysticism. *Là-Bas*, with its monstrous pictures of the Black Mass and the spiritual abominations of Satanism, is one step further in the direction of the supernatural; and it, too, ends desperately: "mais ce siècle se fiche absolument du Christ en gloire; il contamine le surnaturel et vomit l'au-delà." After this there was but one more step to take, and M. Huysmans has taken it. *En Route* is the story of a conversion, and, surely, the strangest story of the strangest conversion that was ever seen. Durtal, the hero of the book, is the same personage whom we have seen in *Là-Bas*, and this personage is neither more nor less than M. Huysmans himself, under the very faintest of disguises. The book makes no pretence to being a novel; it has no incidents save the visit to this church or that, to Saint Sulpice or Saint Séverin, and the ten days' retreat at La Trappe. It is entirely concerned with the history of a soul, and this intense preoccupation has modified even the contours and colours of a style which was the most visible and tangible of any writer of our day. It is true that we get something of the old manner in some of the passages referring to music, to architecture; as, for example, in those wonderful pages in which the cycle of the liturgy is compared to the jewels of the Gothic crown in the Musée de Cluny.

Et le grand Lapidaire avait commencé son œuvre en incrustant, dans ce diadème d'offices, l'hymne de saint Ambroise, et l'invocation tirée de l'Ancien Testament, le " Rorate coeli," ce chant mélancolique de l'attente et de regret, cette gemme fumeuse, violacée, dont l'eau s'éclaire alors qu'après chacune de ses strophes, surgit la déprecation solennelle des patriarches appelant la présence tant espérée du Christ. . . . Et, subitement, sur cette couronne éclatait, après les feux las des Carêmes, l'escarboucle en flamme de la Passion. Sur la suie bouleversée d'un ciel, une croix rouge se dressait et des hourras majestueux et des cris éplorés acclamaient le Fruit ensanglanté de l'arbre; et la "Vexilla regis," se répétait encore, la dimanche suivant, à la férie des Rameaux qui joignait à cette prose de Fortunat l'hymne verte qu'elle accompagnait d'un bruit soyeux de palmes, le "Gloria, laus et honor" de Théodulphe.

But for the most part the language is chastened and constrained into a sort of severity, in which the sharpness and strength of words are used, no longer decoratively, and for their own sakes, but as the most forcible and acute means of expression; demonstrating, indeed, in a particular instance, the exact contrary of this very true general statement: "Non, il n'y a pas à le nier, la complexion de notre race n'est évidemment point ductile à suivre, à expliquer les agissements de Dieu travaillant au centre profond de l'âme, là, où est l'ovaire des penseés, la source même des conceptions; elle est réfractaire à rendre, par la force expressive des mots, le fracas ou le silence de la grâce éclatant dans le domaine ruiné des fautes, inapte à extraire de ce monde secret des œuvres de psychologie, comme celles de sainte Térèse et de saint Jean de la Croix, d'art, comme celles de Voragine ou de la sœur Emmerich." And indeed, in modern French, the book is new; it is a "confession," a self-auscultation of the soul, not in the pleasant and superficial manner of the professed "psychologues," to whom the soul is a dainty cluster of touching and elegant sentiments, but with a certain hard, dry casuistry, a subtlety and a closeness truly ecclesiastical, in the investigation of an obscure and yet definite region, whose intellectual passions are as varied and tumultuous as those of the heart. In this astonishing passage, through Satanism to Faith, in which the cry, "Je suis si las de moi, si dégoûté de ma misérable vie," echoes through page after page, until despair dies into conviction, the conviction of "l'inutilité de se soucier d'autre chose que de la mystique et de la liturgie, de penser à autre chose qu'à Dieu," it is impossible to see a mere exploit of rhetoric, a mere flight of fancy; it has the sincerity of a real, a unique experience. The force of mere curiosity can go far, can penetrate to a certain depth; yet there is a certain point at which mere curiosity, even that of genius, comes to an end; and we are left to the individual soul's apprehension of what seems to it the reality of spiritual things. Such a personal apprehension we cannot but recognize in these words, for instance: " Ce qu'il ressentait, depuis que sa chair le laissait plus lucide, était si insensible, si indéfinissable, si continu pourtant, qu'il devait renoncer à comprendre. En somme, chaque fois qu'il voulait descendre en lui-même, un rideau de brume se levait qui masquait la marche invisible et silencieuse d'il ne savait quoi. La seule impression qu'il rapportait, en remontant, c'est que c'était bien moins lui qui s'avançait dans l'inconnu, que cet inconnu que l'envahissait, le pénétrait, s'emparait, peu à peu, de lui." Such a personal apprehension, again, comes to us, even more unmistakably, in those remarkable pages, near the end of the book, where Durtal enters "la Nuit obscure" of the Catholic mystics, a passage unlike anything else in Huysmans, where, at one point, the very words fail him, and he breaks off with: " Ce fut inexprimable; car rien ne peut rendre les anxiétés, les angoisses de cet état par lequel il faut avoir passé pour le comprendre." Yet, just as, in the days when he forced language to express, in a more coloured and pictorial way than it had ever expressed before, the last escaping details of material things, so, in this analysis of the aberrations and warfares, the confusions and triumphs of the soul in penitence, seeking light and rest, he has found words for even the most subtle and illusive aspects of that inner life which he has come, finally, to apprehend. The book is not an emotional one, much of its strength lies in its sobriety, and certainly much of its curiosity in the ratiocinative tone which pervades it. Every step is taken deliberately, is weighed, approved, condemned, viewed from this side and from that, and at the same time one feels a certain impulsion urging forward this self-analytic soul against its will, in spite of its protests, doubts, and revolts, along a fixed path. The sense of this impelling, this indwelling force, the grace of God, we are led to suppose, is conveyed to us throughout the whole book with an extraordinary skill. The whole book is a sort of thinking aloud; it fixes, in precise words, all the uncertainties, the contradictions, the absurd unreasonableness and not less absurd logic, which distract man's brain in the passing over him of sensation and circumstance. And all this thinking is concentrated on one end, is concerned with the working out, in his own singular way, of one man's salvation. Once again, the conclusion is unsatisfying: " Paris et Notre-Dame-de-l'Atre m'ont rejeté à tour de rôle comme une épave et me voici condamné à vivre dépareillé, car je suis encore trop homme de lettres pour faire un moine et je suis cependant déjà trop moine pour rester parmi des gens de lettres." But the title reminds us that after all this is only *En Route*. What will be the next step, one wonders? Whatever it is, it can hardly fail to be surprising, it can hardly fail to be in some sort logical, for M. Huysmans' development has hitherto been along an ascending spiral, an enigmatical but always ascending spiral of the soul.

A SYMBOLIST FARCE

The performance of *Ubu Roi: comédie guignolesque*, by M. Alfred Jarry, at the Théâtre de l'Œuvre, if of little importance in itself, is of considerable importance as a symptom of tendencies now agitating the minds of the younger generation in France. The play is the first Symbolist farce; it has the crudity of a schoolboy or a savage; what is, after all, most remarkable about it is the insolence with which a young writer mocks at civilization itself, sweeping all art, along with all humanity, into the same inglorious slop-pail. That it should ever have been written is sufficiently surprising; but it has been praised by Catulle Mendès, by Anatole France; the book has gone through several editions, and now the play has been mounted by Lugné-Poe (whose mainly Symbolist Théâtre de l'Œuvre has so significantly taken the place of the mainly Naturalist Théâtre Libre) and it has been given, twice over, before a crowded house, howling but dominated, a house buffeted into sheer bewilderment by the wooden lath of a gross, undiscriminating, infantile Philosopher-Pantaloon.

M. Jarry's idea, in this symbolical buffoonery, was

to satirize humanity by setting human beings to play the part of marionettes, hiding their faces behind cardboard masks, tuning their voices to the howl and squeak which tradition has considerately assigned to the voices of that wooden world, and mimicking the rigid inflexibility and spasmodic life of puppets by a hopping and reeling gait. The author, who has written an essay, *De l'inutilité du théâtre au théâtre*, has explained that a performance of marionettes can only suitably be accompanied by the marionette music of fairs; and therefore, the motions of these puppet-people were accompanied, from time to time, by an orchestra of piano, cymbals, and drums, played behind the scenes, and reproducing the note of just such a band as one might find on the wooden platform outside a canvas booth in a fair. The action is supposed to take place " in Poland, that is to say, in the land of Nowhere "; and the scenery was painted to represent, by a child's conventions, indoors and out of doors, and even the torrid, temperate, and arctic zones at once. Opposite to you, at the back of the stage, you saw apple-trees in bloom, under a blue sky, and against the sky a small closed window and a fireplace, containing an alchemist's crucible, through the very midst of which (with what refining intention, who knows?) trooped in and out these clamorous and sanguinary persons of the drama. On the left was painted a bed, and at the foot of the bed a bare tree, and snow falling. On the right were palm-trees, about one of which coiled a boa-constrictor; a door opened against the sky, and beside the door a skeleton dangled from a gallows. Changes of scene were announced by the simple Elizabethan method of a placard, roughly scrawled with such stage directions as this: "La scène représente la province de Livonie couverte de neige." A venerable gentleman in evening-dress, Father Time as we see him on Christmas-trees, trotted across the stage on the points of his toes between every scene, and hung the new placard on its nail. And before the curtain rose, in what was after all but a local mockery of a local absurdity, two workmen backed upon the stage carrying a cane-bottomed chair and a little wooden table covered with a sack, and M. Jarry (a small, very young man, with a hard, clever face) seated himself at the table and read his own "conférence" on his own play.

In explaining his intentions, M. Jarry seemed to me rather to be explaining the intentions which he ought to have had, or which he had singularly failed to carry out. To be a sort of comic antithesis to Maeterlinck, as the ancient satiric play was at once a pendant and an antithesis to the tragedy of its time: that, certainly, though he did not say it, might be taken to have been one of the legitimate ambitions of the writer of *Ubu Roi*. "C'est l'instauration du Guignol Littéraire," as he affirms, and a generation which has exhausted every intoxicant, every soluble preparation of the artificial, may well seek a last sensation in the wire-pulled passions, the wooden faces of marionettes, and, by a further illusion, of marionettes who are living people; living people pretending to be those wooden images of life which pretend to be living people. There one sees, truly, the excuse, the occasion, for an immense satire, a Swiftian or Rabelaisian parody of the world. But at present M. Jarry has not the intellectual grasp nor the mastery of a new technique needful to carry out so vast a programme. Swift, Rabelais, is above all the satirist with intention, and the satirist who writes. M. Jarry has somehow forgotten his intention before writing, and his writing when he takes pen in hand. *Ubu Roi* is the gesticulation of a young savage of the woods, and it is his manner of expressing his disapproval of civilization. Satire which is without distinctions becomes obvious, and M. Jarry's present conception of satire is very much that of the schoolboy to whom a practical joke is the most efficacious form of humour, and bad words scrawled on a slate the most salient kind of wit. These jerking and hopping, these filthy, fighting, swearing "gamins" of wood bring us back, let us admit, and may legitimately bring us back, to what is primitively animal in humanity. Ubu may be indeed " un sac à vices, une outre à vins, une poche à bile, un empereur romain de la décadence, idoine à toutes cacades, pillard, paillard, braillard, un goulaphre," as the author describes him; but he is not sufficiently that, he is not invented with sufficient profundity, nor set in motion with a sufficiently comic invention. He does not quite attain to the true dignity of the marionette. He remains a monkey on a stick.

Yet, after all, Ubu has his interest, his value; and that strange experiment of the Rue Blanche its importance as a step in the movement of minds. For it shows us that the artificial, when it has gone the full circle, comes back to the primitive; des Esseintes relapses into the Red Indian. M. Jarry is logical, with that frightful, irresistible logic of the French. In our search for sensation we have exhausted sensation; and now, before a people who have perfected the fine shades to their vanishing point, who have subtilized delicacy of perception into the annihilation of the very senses through which we take in ecstasy, a literary Sansculotte has shrieked for hours that unspeakable word of the gutter which was the refrain, the "Leitmotiv," of this comedy of masks. Just as the seeker after pleasure whom pleasure has exhausted, so the seeker after the material illusions of literary artifice turns finally to that first, subjugated, never quite exterminated, element of cruelty which is one of the links which bind us to the earth. *Ubu Roi* is the brutality out of which we have achieved civilization, and those painted, massacring puppets the destroying elements which are as old as the world, and which we can never chase out of the system of natural things.

H. S. NICHOLS, LTD., PRINTERS, 3 SOHO SQUARE, LONDON, W.